100 Selma... *100* Years

by Minnie Belle Phillips, with Patricia Voss

Webster Groves High School
100 Selma Avenue
Webster Groves, MO 63119

Reedy Press
PO Box 5131
St. Louis, MO 63139

Library of Congress Cataloging-in-Publication Data: 2007925605

ISBN: 978-1-933370-00-2
          1-933370-00-9

For all information on all Reedy Press publications
visit our Web site at http://reedypress.com.

Printed in Canada
07   08   09   10   11   5   4   3   2   1

Designed by Bruce Burton

This book is dedicated to the Webster Groves High School community—past, present, and future.

Acknowledgments

100 Selma . . . 100 Years represents a collaborative effort and evolving history from an array of sources: student issues of the *Echo* newspaper, *Echo* annual, and pamphlet series *In Retrospect*; school board scrapbooks, minutes, announcements, and publications; North Webster and Douglass High School memorabilia from the Henrietta Ambrose Papers in the Western Historical Manuscript Collection at the University of Missouri–St. Louis; archival records from the St. Louis Mercantile Library; the personal assistance of James Bieleteldt at the Webster Groves Historical Society; and news stories from the *St. Louis Globe-Democrat*, *St. Louis Post-Dispatch*, and *Webster-Kirkwood Times*.

We are grateful to the Webster Groves High School staff, students, and parents for their encouragement and to the alumni who shared their stories and photographs. Chris Barrett, Daphney Butler, and Casey Caldwell deserve special recognition for their technical assistance. Finally, the Webster Groves Board of Education, Superintendent Brent Underwood, Community Relations Director Cathy Vespereny, and high school Principal Jon Clark supported and aided our research every step of the way.

Table of Contents

Preface

Beginning with a ninth-grade course in 1889 and a new building in 1907, Webster Groves High School emerged as one of the premier high schools in St. Louis County. Much of the school's success stemmed from the foresight of early residents and their cooperation across neighborhood, religious, and racial boundaries to educate youth who often remained in, returned to, or maintained close ties to Webster Groves or surrounding communities.

In 1909, Superintendent Mr. W. D. Grove, declared Webster Groves High School the "people's college": a public secondary school devoted to training in the "higher branches" of learning and preparation of students for a vocational career. James T. Hixson, principal from 1907 to 1943, oversaw the transformation of the village high school to the comprehensive high school. With an ensemble staff consisting of Charles Roberts in mathematics, track, and football; Hazel Farmer in Latin; Helen and Winifred Toner—the "Toner twins"—in mathematics and student activities; Hans Lemcke in instrumental music; Froebel Gaines in boys baseball; Esther Replogle in instrumental music; and Eugene Woods in the dramatic arts, Webster Groves High School rivaled a liberal arts college while achieving scholastic and athletic recognition throughout the state.

Mr. Howard A. Latta, assistant principal under Hixson and high school principal from 1943 to 1968, continued Mr. Hixson's precedent of a strong faculty, rigorous curriculum, and broad student participation during growth in student population after World War II and shifts in student population resulting from the building of junior high schools for grades 7 through 9 and compliance with the 1954 Supreme Court mandate ordering school integration of black and white students.

In the late 1960s, Dr. Gerald S. Kusler, during his brief tenure as principal (1968–69), sought to address the impact of social upheaval on the high school. But it was Mr. Jerry R. Knight who from 1969 to 1986 restored stability during a protracted period of student unrest, population peak and decline, budget constraints, curriculum reorganization, the ninth grade's re-entry, faculty cutbacks, increased federal school legislation and state control, and the district's participation in the St. Louis city–suburban schools voluntary desegregation program.

The late 1980s and 1990s brought a streamlined student population, a succession of principals and faculty intent on improving student achievement and increasing student participation, followed by national publicity and statewide recognition. Dr. Dan Edwards, principal from 1986 to 1992, advanced system-wide technology. Mrs. Yvonne Kauffman, from 1992 to 1995, attempted to increase student enthusiasm. From 1995 to 2003, Ms. Patricia Voss, who since 1969 also served as faculty member, activities director, and assistant principal, renewed school pride and prepared the high school for the national spotlight, featuring visits by President Bill Clinton in 1998 and *Sports Illustrated* and *Time* magazine in 1999.

The year 2003–2004 brought Dr. Jon Clark as principal and increases in parent involvement, staff leadership, student achievement, minority student participation, athletic successes, school pride, updated technology, and state recognition.

Webster Groves High School today bears little resemblance to the six-room school that opened with 120 students in the fall of 1907. Yet the school's dedicated staff, supportive parents and community, and student accomplishments in academics, the arts, interscholastic contests, athletics, and community service continue to fulfill Superintendent W. D. Grove's promise of an exemplary public high school.

100 Selma . . . 100 Years is a compilation of stories and images of a high school within a close-knit community, of a school embodying and transcending the legacies and successes of students, alumni, and staff, and of a school intent on the future while preserving the past.

Early History

The Bristol School housed the Webster Groves School District's first high school.

The rise of the public high school in the late nineteenth century found fertile soil in Webster Groves. The quiet St. Louis suburb with its rural roots, small-town culture, and civic-minded leadership provided an ideal location to prepare students for the shift from an agricultural to an industrialized and technological society away from the "distractions" of the city. As early as 1868, the newly organized Webster Groves School District provided public elementary education for white children at Bristol Grammar School on Gray Avenue and for black children at Douglass School in North Webster.

In 1889, the School Board began its first efforts to provide secondary education. Miss Sarah J. Milligan was hired to teach a ninth-grade course on the first floor of the Bristol School while serving as principal of the school and eventually superintendent of the system. By 1891, the "Webster Groves High School Department" offered a two-year program, with two teachers assisting Ms. Milligan. Students wishing to continue their education beyond Bristol took the train at the Tuxedo Depot or traveled by horse and buggy to St. Louis City.

The early high school graduated its first class of only three students on February 2, 1900. Commencement exercises were held at the First Congregational Church, and graduates included Mary Adelaide Howe, Mary Widmann, and Millie Widmann.

Mr. Mark Moody, a graduate of the high school, served as the second principal of the high school department, followed by Mr. Charles Thurston, and Mr. George L. Hawkins. When enrollment outgrew its space at Bristol School, classes in 1901 moved to the third floor of the old Bristol Building, a multi-use retail and community center on Lockwood and in 1904 through 1906 to the old Brennan Building north of the Missouri-Pacific railroad tracks on Gore.

Since 1901, the Webster Groves School Board had petitioned voters to pass a bond issue for a new high school. Critics questioned public funding for schooling beyond eighth grade. Others claimed they had succeeded without a high school education. The civic core persevered, and in 1905, after two defeats, voters approved a $40,000 bond issue to purchase a site and build a high school at the corner of Selma and Bradford.

The broom bridgade was one of the high school's first co-curricular activities.

Selma Avenue, on April 27, 1906, offered a dreary view for students, teachers, school officials, and guest speaker Dr. Louis Soldan, superintendent of the St. Louis Public Schools, invited to the cornerstone ceremony. Wooden planks formed shaky sidewalks, and the muddy road along the site proved a quagmire for horse-drawn wagons and hapless automobiles trapped in downpours. The field across from the school offered a pond ringed by willows but no neighboring houses.

Still, the "central school building" united the community. The two-story brick high school, when completed, would contain three classrooms and an office on the first floor, an auditorium doubling as a study hall on the second floor, and two storerooms in the basement.

High school enrollment had risen from 74 students in 1902 to nearly 150 students in 1907. Four students graduated in 1902, seven in 1903, four in 1904, seven in 1905, eleven in 1906, and fifteen in 1907. Non-resident students from Clayton and Maplewood attended Webster Groves High School on a tuition basis.

The new high school at 100 Selma opened in 1907 under the leadership of the newly hired James Hixson. Hixson served as principal of the high school for thirty-seven years, making a profound effect on the direction and character of the school as we know it.

Part I

THE HIXSON ERA

Chapter 1

> *"In that year, there were six teachers including myself. I taught six classes. Then the seventh grade from Bristol Grammar School was in with us, and in all we had between one hundred twenty and thirty pupils."*
>
> —James Hixson

James T. Hixson, the "Foundation of Webster Groves High School," was hired as principal in 1907. The soft-spoken leader embraced Webster Groves as his home and treated its children as his own by nurturing the intellectual, aesthetic, and spiritual growth of his students. In turn, his thoughtful decisions and tireless efforts on behalf of the school endeared him to the faculty and the community.

Mr. Hixson's small-town background proved a fruitful match with Webster Groves. He grew up in Marshall, Missouri, in the northeastern part of the state, where he attended Missouri Valley College, a Presbyterian liberal arts school. He worked in rural schools in Marshall and Memphis, Missouri, where he served as principal and superintendent, before accepting the position of principal at the little high school on Selma Avenue.

During the "Hixson Era," from 1907 to 1943, Webster Groves High School became one of the most prominent high schools in St. Louis County. The steady climb in enrollment resulted in broader course offerings, a distinguished faculty, and rebuilding cycles through the first three decades of the twentieth century. The faculty of six in 1907 grew to twenty-seven by 1927. The number of graduates over the same period grew from 15 to 120. By 1935, enrollment reached over 1,700 students in grades 7 through 12. In 1940, the senior class stood at 240, sixteen times the number earning diplomas at the new high school's first commencement.

Mr. James T. Hixson was for thirty-seven years the symbol of the spirit that is Webster Groves High School.

BUILDING EXPANSIONS

Building changes in the early decades stemmed from suburban growth and student increases as well as trends in public education philosophy. Manual training and domestic sciences rooms were completed in the basement in 1909. Two wings were added to the front of the building in 1914. The left (south) wing housed the Webster Groves High School Gymnasium, and the right (north) wing held an auditorium, twelve classrooms, and a girls' gymnasium. On the second floor, the walls partitioning three classrooms serving as lunch rooms were removed to open more space, and science rooms were also added.

facing page: The Class of 1921 gathers for their freshmen picture.

By 1924, the original building had been remodeled and expanded several times but was soon to be replaced by a building large enough to handle grades 7 through 12.

The 1924 *Echo* describes Frank Hamsher as a man whose personal life formed the basis of his power. He was intellectually honest, broad-minded, tolerant, kind-hearted, pure of heart, a true friend, and a visionary.

In 1917, an Armory on the Bradford Avenue side of the high school was built for the home guard—volunteers replacing troops activated during the war. Since the guard only drilled once or twice a week, the high school was able to use the Armory for indoor track, basketball practices, and graduation exercises. After the war, the building was turned over to the School Board, and the basement was dug out and converted to a lunchroom. The building was razed in 1944 and replaced with a senior high gymnasium.

The high school underwent major renovations from 1924 to 1928. The passage of a $174,800 bond issue in December 1925 provided funding to complete the second section of the high school, which allowed senior high students to occupy the new building and junior high students to occupy the old building.

A 1927 bond issue funded completion of an auditorium, girls' gymnasium, and nine new classrooms. The new Frank Hamsher High School formally opened on October 6, 1927, and honored the district's fourth superintendent, who died in 1924. Bristol students contributed the money for the plaque in Mr. Hamsher's memory, and the Bristol PTA presented the bronze tablet on the wall near the display case of the senior entrance with Mr. Hamsher's last remarks: "To keep your life pure, choose good companions. When in trouble, turn to God."

The next round of changes came in the 1930s, when the original school, used for the junior high, was torn down and rebuilt to relieve overcrowding and to eliminate fire hazards. In 1931, the Frank Hamsher High School and the junior high were consolidated into a six-year high school and dedicated on March 11, 1935. The "new" modern Webster Groves High School contained twenty-eight rooms, two gymnasiums, vocal and instrumental practice rooms, a model Little Theater, foods

The new public library on the campus of Webster Groves High School was financed and constructed by a grant from the Works Progress Administration, a federal program during the Franklin Roosevelt presidency.

and clothing laboratories, art rooms, and a public library. The school enrolled 269 seventh graders, 315 eighth graders, 307 ninth graders, 278 tenth graders, 291 eleventh graders, and 244 twelfth graders, for a total of 1,704 students. The school boasted two modern wings of its senior and junior high divisions, bridged by a public library.

CURRICULUM CHANGES

The school day in 1907 began at 9:00 a.m. and ended at 2:30 p.m. Students exercised little freedom over course selections, geared to a four-year program of "Scientific" or "Classical" studies. Courses included English, Latin, French, German, history, science, and mathematics. German classes were suspended during World War I, but they resumed afterwards, with one year of German in junior high and the second year in senior high. Spanish was added in 1917. Biology later replaced general science.

Manual training or "shop" (woodworking and mechanical drawing) and "domestic sciences" or home economics (cooking and sewing) were added to the curriculum in 1909. Chemistry was added in 1913. Physical training for girls was added in 1914; girls were required to wear bloomers and long stockings to cover their legs. A commercial department offering typing, shorthand, and bookkeeping was added in 1915.

Physical education for women had as its goal the development of health, beauty, and grace. It included work in aesthetics, folk dance, running, fancy steps, Indian clubs, and dumbbells.

English, social studies, mathematics, physical education, and science constituted the core curriculum, but by the 1930s, the march toward a comprehensive high school included vocal and instrumental music, civics, economics, and dramatics as popular electives. In 1935, Webster Groves High School offered forty-five courses for students in grades 10 through 12.

The co-curricular program had its beginnings in the early Greek literary societies. These groups spawned the newspaper, yearbook, debate club, and dramatic productions.

Having been razzed by the opposing team's fans for their lack of cheerleaders, the men of the Class of 1922 organized the Razzers, Webster's first cheerleading squad. The Razzers appeared at football and basketball games to generate fan support for the Statesmen.

Sixteen and a half credits were required for graduation. A college entrance-level diploma required four years of English, two years of history, two years of foreign language, three years of mathematics, one year of science, and three years of physical education. Students chose from an array of electives, including sociology, stagecraft, and public speaking. Extracurricular activities consisted of school clubs, honor societies, and publications, most of which met during school hours.

STUDENT ACTIVITIES AND ORGANIZATIONS

Webster Groves held to its tradition of reinforcing the home-church-school connection, but it left much of the cultural and social life of its teenagers to school clubs and organizations. Virtually every student during the school's first two decades belonged to a club, the earliest literary Greek societies sponsoring talks, recitals, debates, creative writing, readings, and guest speakers on topics ranging from the classics to current events. The Papyrus Club, Athenian Club, Delphi Club, Philomathian Club, Arena Club, Dramatic Club, and Debating Club spawned a proliferation of organizations to supplement the curriculum, to cultivate self-expression, and to encourage student initiative and responsibility.

Student Council began in October 1927, operating through homeroom delegates. The Dean's Council—starting with seventeen girls—aimed to "promote the highest ideals in scholastic and social life of the school." The Advisory Board—predominately boys—assumed legislative and administrative functions of student government.

By the 1930s, Student Council developed into a seasoned organization, committed to serving as "a mouthpiece for student ideas" and promoting communication and cooperation between students and the administration. In the "lower school" (junior high), the organization created a student jury and hall-monitoring system, assuming a leadership role in student discipline.

The Student Council's Activities Committee not only planned student activities but also resolved scheduling conflicts. The Council's Student Award Board bestowed a service pin to ten students each year who earned the highest number of points for their work in extracurricular activities.

Clubs drew on student interests to foster awareness, showcase talent, and revive school spirit. The foreign language clubs *Le Cercle Francais, El Club Espanol,* and *Conventus Latinus* presented plays, parodies, charades, musical selections, dances, reports, and speeches at meetings and school assemblies. The Latin Club grew out of Latin classes, long a staple at the high school and the province of Miss Hazel Farmer. The German Club, *Der Deutsche Verein,* organized in 1936.

Senior, junior, sophomore, and freshmen dramatic clubs concentrated on playwriting, acting, and directing. There was also a reading club, poetry club, science club, radio club, career club, gymnastics club, Hi-Y (high school YMCA and YWCA) Christian life and service club, girls' glee club, and later boys' glee club. The MacDowell Club celebrated "the artistry and altruism of the American composer Edward MacDowell." The Splashe Shoppe Club, an arm of the "W" athletic club, made artful signs and posters to advertise sports and social events throughout the school.

The Creative Writing Club organized to cultivate literary talent. The Fencing Club, with the encouragement of dramatic and girls' coach Miss Dorothy Stanley, organized in 1931, as did the Aviation Club, to promote an interest in aeronautics by planning visits to airplane factories and nearby airfields. The Photography Club, known as the "Kodak Club" because of their interest in taking ordinary snapshots, organized in 1931. The Library Staff Club consisted of student volunteers from the junior and senior class.

The Yellow Jackets were the forerunners of the girls' cheerleading squads. They organized to promote "clean athletics, good sportsmanship, and a feeling of fellowship among all the girls in the upper school" (senior high) as well as to increase enthusiasm for school activities and to boost school spirit throughout the school.

By the 1940s, student clubs ranged from serious action groups to recreational interests. The Pan American League promoted awareness in South American affairs, while the Social Action Committee, which published its own magazine, *The Question Mark,* tackled pressing local, state, and national issues such as civil rights, poverty, unemployment, and war. The Roller Skating Club met at the Maplewood Rink to earn Girls Athletic Association points and to promote camaraderie. The Ping Pong Club organized in 1941 as an intramural and intra-scholastic sport, and with seventy members became one of the school's largest clubs.

"Unofficial" publications preceded official student publications. Morris Mathis, a student of the early high school before Selma, remembered that there was a student newspaper named *Snide Herald* containing mostly jokes. Underground newspapers would surface again in the late 1960s, but Webster Groves High School's publishing tradition had already taken root.

The senior class of 1911 produced the first yearbook, *The Senior,* while the sophomore class published the first *Echo* newspaper on December 20, 1915. With the *Echo,* students promised "to present the thoughts, ideas and feelings of the pupils" and "to reveal to the outside world their literary ability." George Massengale, class of 1918, was the first *Echo* editor and recalled that there

Clubs at Webster developed from student interests. The boys' Skating Club of 1935 sought to help students learn to skate or improve their skating skills.

On Monday afternoon, the girls gathered to skate at the Winter Garden. Weather permitting, the group skated on the "lakes" in the area.

Membership in the Joseph Pulitzer Chapter of Quill and Scroll required junior status, a rank in the upper third of the class and a position on the school paper or yearbook.

was a staff of eight students, with no sponsor, and the paper was censored by the editor in chief. The goal of producing one issue a month was hampered by lack of time, guidance, and assistance, since there was no journalism class and no class period set aside for production.

In February 1916, the *Echo* newspaper earned its first profit by selling and publishing the advertisements of local merchants. Beginning in 1917, the staff comprised students from different classes, in grades 10 through 12. By 1923, the paper had its first sponsor, Miss Mary Howard, an English teacher, serving as advisor for both the newspaper and the yearbook before the staffs separated in 1924.

The *Echo* became a charter member of Quill and Scroll, the national (and later international) honorary society for high school journalists, in May 1927, a year after George H. Gallup established the organization at the University of Iowa. That same year, the *Echo* became a charter member of the National Scholastic Press Association, a remarkable feat given that none of the writers had journalism training. In 1936, the *Echo* staff was awarded the Silver Loving Cup at Washington University for the best overall high school newspaper in St. Louis.

The high school's forensics fame began with speech and debate teacher Mr. Julian C. Aldrich, a University of Chicago graduate with degrees in history, philosophy, and law. In 1926, the school became a charter member of the National Forensic League based on its outstanding achievement in debate, extemporaneous speaking, original oratory, and dramatic declamation. In 1933, the Webster Groves Chapter of the Forensic League was the first to win the Distinguished Service Award for outstanding achievement in forensics (and the only chapter to win it a second time). Mr. Aldrich was the first recipient of the Distinguished Service Key, the highest award given to an individual honoree.

The 1927 Debate Club, under the direction of Mr. Aldrich, participated in a variety of forensic activities, and students traveled to William Woods and Westminster College for tournaments.

The high school emerged as a debate powerhouse in the 1930s. Twenty-six students were members of the Debate Squad in 1934, the largest group ever at Webster High. In 1938, the high school's Forensic League was the only group to win all of its State League District debates and the only high school to be represented in all national tournaments. Debate topics ranged from the Monroe Doctrine, to the Unicameral State Legislative System, to centralized control of industry, to equal rights for men and women, as students debated throughout Missouri and at midwestern universities.

Chemistry teacher William Louis "Doc" Schulz sponsored the Chemistry Club, whose purpose was to advance the knowledge of chemistry and to explore its practical applications. Weekly meetings were used for demonstrations or experiments benefiting future laboratory scientists.

The Torch, the Webster Groves High School Chapter of the National Honor Society, received its charter in 1935 and inducted thirty-nine members. Eligibility requirements for seniors and juniors included faculty review and qualification based on four criteria: scholarship, leadership, character, and service.

Every year in late April or early May, more than 100 Webster Groves High School students took trains or drove to the University of Missouri–Columbia for statewide interscholastic contests. The high school frequently earned first or second place in English, mathematics (advanced algebra), Latin, public speaking, and debate.

General science gave way to biology and chemistry. The 1911 senior men prepare for a lab experiment in chemistry.

Candidates for the *Echo* Queen were selected from the senior class and voted on by the students of the upper school.

The National Thespians Chapter, the honorary dramatics society, organized in 1931. The first initiates were leads in school plays and later included such behind-the-scenes "actors" as business managers, house managers, property managers, and publicity managers. In 1933, the high school's Thespians Chapter raised initiation requirements beyond national standards to limit membership to students most active in dramatics. Still, by 1935, more than 100 students had become Thespians.

The close of each school year brought a whirlwind of activities, including the highly anticipated selection of the *Echo* Queen (elected by yearbook subscribers) and coronation of the May Queen (chosen by girls of the senior high). The customary dances, banquets, luncheons, and receptions were held for students, athletes, faculty, and seniors. These events during the early years were held at the Bristol Building, with its "polished floors and pennanted walls," or in Emmanuel Episcopal Church's large reading room, with its lush ferns and soft music.

The senior play—whether farcical or serious—was the crowning performance of the graduating class, which rented costumes and hired an electrician to handle electrical details and a professional makeup artist to apply "paint and powder." "Commencement Week" included a baccalaureate sermon, Class Night (for the senior play and dance), Class Day, Junior Reception (for the seniors), and finally graduation exercises. By the 1930s, the senior prom—planned by the junior class—was a school tradition, as was the parting gift of the graduating class.

In 1936, high school seniors received scholarships to Smith College, Mount Holyoke, and Harvard University in Massachusetts; Rockford College in Illinois; Cornell University in New York; and William Jewell, Westminister, and Drury College in Missouri. The largest percentage of Webster Groves High School graduates chose Washington University in St. Louis and the University of Missouri–Columbia.

In a special assembly, Miss Dolly Ann Yost, Class of 1933, was crowned *Echo* Queen.

Chapter 2

> *"The object of all athletics is not so much that we win, but the enjoyment derived and the development of intellect and body into useful citizens."*
>
> —Charles Roberts, 1911

Girls' athletics organized before boys' athletics when a group of girls in 1902 formed the first high school basketball team, coached by Miss Amanda Adams, and played St. Louis's Central High School. The team lasted one season but paved the way for the Girls Athletic Association (GAA). Founded in 1922, the GAA offered membership to any girl playing a school sport or receiving a class letter. In 1928, the organization awarded letters during its annual banquet to an undefeated basketball team. In 1929, the association adopted as its insignia a diamond-shaped pin with the orange letters GAA against a black enamel background to commemorate team fellowship. Among the association's traditions, aside from the annual banquet, was sponsoring the annual "Backward Dance," in which girls invited boys to the dance, which ended with the crowning of the "Kampus King."

By the late 1920s, girls' participation in basketball, tennis, baseball, track, field hockey, fencing, and modern dance was well under way, in large part due to Miss Dorothy Stanley. The physical education teacher and girls' coach arrived in 1925, and by 1927, the *Echo* paid her this tribute: "She has striven to hold before the girls high standards of sportsmanship, and through her work and personality has become not only a leader but a friend of her pupils."

The girls' basketball team played Nerinx Hall, Kirkwood, University City, Wellston, Clayton, Principia, Maplewood, and Mary Institute. The baseball team played Ritenour, University City, Hancock, Wellston, and Ferguson. The field hockey team played at Mary Institute.

The school's orange and black colors were chosen in 1902, the legacy of Mark Moody, graduate of the first high school class and alumnus of Princeton, whose orange and black school colors he borrowed. Moody recalled that the first stirrings of boys' athletics began with football and other sports in 1903. There were no eligibility requirements and no designated playing field. Players were sometimes recruited from the male faculty, boys from other schools, local citizens, or almost anyone wanting to play and furnish his own uniform.

The football team played two games against Ferguson High School, one game against Kirkwood High, one against Marion-Sims College's second team, and one against Smith Academy, a private

Ruth Bailey, 1927 tennis star, won the Mississippi Valley and Women's Championship Cup and completed her year with a state championship in singles.

facing page: Organized in 1922, the GAA provided an opportunity for the young women of WGHS to participate in basketball, baseball, track, and tennis.

The 1919 GAA basketball team finished the season 8–1, losing to Clayton by one point. The girls received fudge and flowers from their ardent fans.

Constantly looking for opportunities for women to take part in athletic competition, the GAA organized a women's rifle team.

boys' high school connected with Washington University. They were victorious in all these contests except Marion-Sims, a medical training college affiliated with the Saint Louis University School of Medicine. During the winter, Webster High School boys formed a hockey team, again with an assortment of players.

WEBSTER-KIRKWOOD RIVALRY

During the 1920s, the Webster Groves football Statesmen considered Clayton High School their "ancient rival" and Maplewood High School a "tough adversary," but it was the Thanksgiving "Turkey Day" game against its neighbor, Kirkwood High School, that led to the oldest continuous high school football rivalry west of the Mississippi River.

The competition began in 1907, despite some speculation that the two teams played against each other as early as 1903. The rules and team organization were different in those days. Each game had the usual four quarters of fifteen minutes, but a touchdown counted for five points instead of six. There were reserve players but no separation into offensive and defensive squads, since the same players played the whole time. There was no place kick. Teams drop kicked or punted. There was little passing, and runners mostly plunged for the line.

The boys dressed in the basement before playing on the athletic field behind the high school, which was barely large enough to accommodate two teams of eleven players. Football gear was light compared to today's heavy padding, but the game was just as rugged. The cheerleaders were all males, and the girls gleefully rooted along the sidelines.

In an interview reported in *In Retrospect*, a 1975 high school local history class publication, Scott Smith, a freshman injured in the first game against Kirkwood, reported that the two sides were out for clean, rough fun in a battle of brawn and will:

> Our motto was, "Hit them hard and tell them nothing." I had an accident in the first game. . . . I still have the mark. I caught the ball on the kick-off. Kirkwood had a big team and there I was, same size as I am now (5'7") a little under that, but I caught the ball and I was a good runner. I started tearing down the field when I saw a man, who looked to me like a giant, one of the Kirkwood fellas, who weighed every bit of 225 pounds, come charging at me. I tried to duck him. The ground was frozen hard and that fella hit me below the knees. Before I realized what had happened, my nose hit the hard frozen ground. See, it's broken. That's my mark of high school.

There was no Friendship Dance, no school decorations, no pep rally, no bonfire, no tickets, no marching band, no Little Brown Jug for the loser, and no Frisco Bell for the winner. These traditions came later. There was simply hard-fought football with no aftermath.

While Webster, according to Kirkwood player John Geppert, had bigger players, the Webster winning tradition did not start until 1910, when the rules changed and the contest stiffened. The score, for unknown reasons, was not reported in 1911, and the two teams did not compete in 1914 and 1918 because of the war. Neither did they play from 1924 to 1927 due to cancellations stemming from bitterness following the 1923 game, when referees reversed the Pioneers' three touchdowns and incited violent protests by some Kirkwood fans. Still, during the first twenty years of competition,

Packed stands and hard-fought battles are the hallmark of the annual Turkey Day game.

Webster won nine of thirteen games. The Kirkwood Pioneers didn't rally until 1930, when they won consecutive victories from 1930 to 1934, before the Statesmen hit their stride with their own five-year winning streak.

One of the early heroes of Turkey Day lore was Allen Lincoln, a Statesmen "titan" playing in the 1917 game. Fleet-footed and weighing two-hundred pounds, "Big Lincoln" was a triple star in football, basketball, and track. Not only did Webster Groves defeat Kirkwood 76–0 that year, but Lincoln also reportedly outplayed Washington University's freshmen and varsity players during his junior and senior years at Webster Groves High School. Later, at age twenty, he was voted All-American while playing football at the University of Missouri–Columbia.

Few people in the early decades recognized the magnitude of the Webster-Kirkwood Turkey Day game, but by the 1930s the game was turning into an event. The Webster Hi-Y (the high school affiliate of the YMCA) in 1934 sponsored the first "Friendship Dance," held after Thanksgiving (instead of before, as now) to restore harmony between the two schools. The highlight of the dance was the crowning of each school's football queens. At first there were "interchange" or progressive dances—three dances in one—in which Webster boys danced with Kirkwood girls,

A three-sports athlete, Allen Lincoln, class of 1918, was Webster Groves High School's first college All-American.

Jane Clemons descends from the throne after being crowned football queen for 1938.

Kirkwood boys danced with Webster girls, then couples or partners from the same school danced with each other.

The marching band debuted in 1937. Called the "Regimental Band," the athletic band was voluntary and offered no course credit. Mr. Pete Myers, high school art teacher and drum and bugle corps enthusiast, formed the precision band, backed by a strong percussion ensemble. The band was among the first in St. Louis County to use field formation and complex maneuvers. On Turkey Day, after three weeks of night rehearsal, the band marched up Lockwood to City Hall and back, led by cheerleaders, a drum major, and a baton twirler. At halftime, the band formed the letter K for Kirkwood and W for Webster and played each school's alma mater.

The Kirkwood and Webster Hi-Y chapters began the Little Brown Jug tradition as a light-hearted gesture toward the loser. The score was etched on the jug, and the captain of the winning team gave the captain of the losing team the jug as a token of a game well played. Eventually, the jug conjured up images of drunken dissolution and was scrapped in favor of the Frisco Bell.

The new Turkey Day "trophy" arrived in 1952, after Kirkwood's principal, Mr. Murl Moore, received the bell as a gift from a friend, Bob Stone, who was vice president of the Frisco Railroad. Stone offered Moore a brass bell from a steam locomotive, since the company was replacing its steam engines with diesel units. Stone knew of the football rivalry between Kirkwood and Webster and figured the bell would make a unique and imposing trophy.

The first year the bell was available to be awarded, the game ended in a 0–0 tie. Webster won the bell in 1953 and 1954. Stone sent the 400-pound bell by carriage to Kirkwood High School in 1952, but the bell—for over fifty years—traveled back and forth for a year's display in the winning team's school. The student councils at both schools were in charge of presentations to the winning captain after each Turkey Day game, and the bell was rung throughout the school day the following Monday. Otherwise, the ringer was removed for each school's sanity.

The Turkey Day game remains legendary in the St. Louis area and the rivalry remains as fierce on the field as it is friendly in Webster Groves, Kirkwood, and neighboring communities. Thousands of alumni and residents still race to attend the game on Thanksgiving Day, and perhaps no one would be more surprised at the spectacle and the frenzy than the rough hewn teams playing the first game in 1907.

CHARLES ROBERTS AND FROEBEL GAINES

If for three decades Webster Groves High School was synonymous with James T. Hixson, then the school's track, football, and basketball programs belonged to Charlie Roberts, and its baseball program belonged to Froebel Gaines. Coach Roberts groomed young men and women to "lead the field." Together, he and Gaines ushered in the Statesmen championship and sportsmanship tradition.

Roberts did not bring athletics to Webster Groves, but he instilled a fierce pride, loyalty, and fighting spirit in his players. By the time he died of a heart attack short of his fortieth year at the high school, he had produced an array of champion athletes. Roberts Gym at Webster Groves High School stands as a tribute to the coach, but before he became a legend, Alvah W. Clayton, Class of 1915, wrote this description of his mathematics teacher, coach, and mentor in the Senior annual:

He is admirable on the athletic field as well as in the school room. He wins, and has always won, the admiration and love of every boy, whether the boy be an aspiring contestant or enthusiastic onlooker of all athletic events. His comic and forceful expressions of "go like a bullet," and "hit him and turn him over end," give life and encouragement to every player on the gridiron. The mere knowledge that this honored coach is present at any game forces every player to do his duty to the best of his ability. However dark the prospects for a winning team may appear, he never fails to bring his group of veterans and greenhorns to the front ranks, face to face with victory. His ability to execute all sports in the cleverest fashion gains the pride and amazement of everyone, boy or girl.

Charles Roberts, like James T. Hixson, came to Webster Groves High School in September 1907. Also like Hixson, he was calm and thoughtful in his approach to students. Roberts attended Northeast State College in Kirksville (formerly Kirksville Normal School), in upstate Missouri, and was hired at Webster Groves High School to teach mathematics and coach track and football. Later, he added basketball, baseball, and the rifle team to his coaching duties before becoming athletic director.

The first track team organized in 1905, two years before Roberts came to Webster Groves. The first coach the Statesmen had was, as Roberts described him, "a tall, big red-haired fellow" who moved to Great Falls, Montana. Also, since there was no track at the high school, boys had to take a streetcar to Washington University to practice at Francis Field.

Roberts became track coach in 1907. Under his direction, Webster Groves High School teams won meets throughout the region, and Roberts' legacy as the creator of champions began. The first track star was Henry Theilecke, whose specialty was the broad jump. Reportedly, when "Heine" jumped at the Mississippi Valley Meet, he would jump only once, and since no once could top his record, he considered his day's work done and refused to jump again.

Another star athlete was big Allen Lincoln, formidable in football and basketball as well as track. Roberts called Lincoln "a team within himself." Lincoln was only a sophomore in 1917 at the state track meet when he won the 100- and 200-yard dash, the broad jump, the discus throw, placed third in the shot put, and led his relay team to victory.

In 1918, George Massengale—track champion and *Echo* editor—starred in the days when there were no facilities for either track practice or newspaper production. Massengale was a standout in high school but soared at the University of Missouri when he broke the 220-yard dash world record in 1920 at the Chicago Relays and won a slot on the United States Olympic team.

By 1926, the boys track team had won the St. Louis County championship twenty-six consecutive times as well as two consecutive Mississippi Valley Interscholastic championships. Webster Groves High School didn't dominate track records again until Ivory Crockett's feat as the "fastest runner in the world" in 1968.

Roberts' football Statesmen were labeled the "County Champions" because of their relentlessly hard

The Little Brown Jug was annually presented to the captain of the losing team following the Turkey Day game. This jug is one of three which records the scores across the decades.

To the victor, goes the BELL!

The Class of 1920 dedicated their yearbook to Charles Roberts in appreciation of his fine work both on the athletic field and in the classroom.

This 1919 *Echo* cartoon shows the mighty Webster tiger crushing all of its opponents, whether football, basketball, or track. The tiger was the previous Webster mascot.

play, rousing school support, and cumulative winning seasons. The 1915 team played Maplewood, Rankin, Ferguson, St. Charles, Kirkwood, and Smith-Manual, with only one loss—to Smith-Manual, a private boys' school with a "much heavier team."

The *Echo* annual described the Statesmen 1924 football season as "a season of upsets, of joy and gloom, of brilliant performances and an unbelievable slump." Roberts reportedly had made a "real scrapping team" of the fifty boys who showed up for practice before the beginning of the season. The team played University City, East St. Louis, Normandy, McKinley, Ritenour, Maplewood, and Clayton, suffering only two defeats, one from its alumni squad and another from University City, to finish second in the county.

Francis Field at Washington University was the site of the 1911 State track meet.

In 1926–27, Joe Lintzenich was a football legend and one of few Webster Groves alumni to play professional sports. Lintzenich, along with Bud Sample, led a virtually unbeatable Statesmen team. Like Allen Lincoln the decade before him, Lintzenich was a triple champion, lettering in track, baseball, and football. He was the star punter in football, once reportedly kicking the ball from his end zone and setting the opposing team back eighty-five yards. Following graduation, Lintzenich played for Saint Louis University, where he was captain of the football team. Afterwards, he played for the Chicago Bears, for whom he kicked the second-longest punt in NFL history, at 94 yards.

Statesmen basketball presented similar scenarios. From 1914 to 1931, Coach Roberts' basketball teams had two perfect seasons, in 1915–16 and 1918–19, and only one losing season, in 1927–28. The 1916–17 team traveled to Chicago to play in a national tournament of thirty-five of the country's top basketball teams. Again, Allen Lincoln, as he had done in football and track, led the 1917 and 1918 basketball teams to victory.

The Statesmen tennis team had occupied a place near the top since the early years. The Rifle Team had organized by 1915 and won eight victories in eleven years of county championships, including five consecutive victories from 1922 to 1926. The team's county rival was Maplewood High School and in the city, Grover Cleveland High School. Golf came later when Webster Groves High School students played in their first tournament in 1928 and organized a golf team in 1933.

The "W" Club was organized in 1917 for the purpose of awarding letters in track, football, baseball, basketball, and shooting at its annual banquet for "high school boys and their fathers." By 1924, the high school's athletic roster included football, tennis, basketball, swimming, baseball, rifling, and track. Membership requirements added in 1929 included playing 60 percent of the games, signing a no-smoking and no-drinking pledge, practicing three times a week, going to bed by 10:30 the night before a game, and obtaining the coach's recommendations.

Webster Groves High School dominated track for twenty-six consecutive years, with Bud Sample among its stars.

After the Missouri High School Athletic Association (MHSAA) formed in 1926, Webster Groves High School found itself restricted by new rules governing who and whom they played. The association's stated objectives were to promote sportsmanship, standardize eligibility rules, "promote the interests of its members," and regulate competition between schools. Webster Groves High School's hesitation in joining the state organization came from the school's desire to continue playing in the County League as well as schools in the city. After these conditions were met, at least for the remainder of 1926, Webster Groves High School became a member of the State Athletic League.

The 1915–1916 perfect season was one of two for Coach Roberts in basketball.

In 1928, the high school became a charter member of the National Interscholastic Athletic Association. The University of Chicago, host of the yearly National Interscholastic Basketball Tournament and the National Interscholastic Track and Field Meet, organized this association.

FROEBEL GAINES

For years, baseball was considered the weakest link of Webster Groves High School boys' athletics. In the spring of 1928, the team had reason for hope. Froebel Gaines, their new coach, scheduled eighteen games—twice as many as the team had every played in a season. The line-up included Eden, Hancock, Soldan, Ritenour, Central, Kirkwood, Wellston, Roosevelt, Cleveland, Jennings, Normandy, Maplewood, Beaumont, and Belleville. The larger schedule meant more playing time and experience, and over the next thirty years the "Gainesmen" often dominated the Suburban League title.

Coach Gaines proved himself an athlete long before coming to Webster Groves High School in 1926. An Illinois boy, he played baseball at Sidell Township High School, Millikin University, and at the University of Illinois. For twelve years he taught geography and coached varsity baseball at Webster Groves High School. He also began coaching varsity football in 1932 but returned to coaching sophomore "B" football in 1937.

Coach Froebel Gaines's seventeen seasons at WGHS produced 397 victories and 147 losses in varsity baseball, and 121 victories and 16 losses in sophomore football.

Rarely boastful, Gaines admitted years later in a January 18, 1959, interview, "I played baseball against the best pitcher in the National League in 1905—Joe McGinnity—and I played against the best in the National League in 1955—Robin Roberts," when Gaines played against the future baseball star in 1945. "I played regularly," Gaines added. "I finished with a .342 batting average and the last baseball game I ever played I hit five doubles in a row and stole 11 bases."

Poker-faced and fun-loving, with a sly humor, "Froeb," as he was affectionately called by his players, was an athlete, soldier, teacher, coach, and scholar—the proverbial "officer and a gentleman." He served two years in the Armed Forces in World War I and forty-four months in the Navy in World War II, leaving the Navy a full commander and returning to Webster Groves High School to resume his coaching career. He also earned a master's degree at the University of Colorado and completed doctoral work at the University of Oregon.

The W Club, the honorary athletic society of Webster High, awards letters to the year's outstanding athletes at their annual banquet.

Coach Gaines's mental, physical, and leadership prowess manifested itself on the athletic field. He preferred coaching the underdogs—younger athletes and inexperienced teams—and transforming them into champions. His record remained enviable at Webster Groves High School, considering that he lingered in the shadow of Coach Roberts. Yet over his seventeen seasons of coaching, "Froeb" marshaled 397 victories and 147 losses in varsity baseball and 121 victories and 16 defeats in sophomore football.

Chapter 3

"We must seek to make music important to the lives of the students participating and to those who listen. It cannot be entertainment alone. Music must be an emotional release, an aesthetic experience. Music must add immeasurable to the cultural life of all of the people and provide an educational discipline in its wake."
—Hans Lemcke, 1953

The arts were hardly new at Webster Groves High School in the 1920s. From 1907 to 1925, Miss Martha Kendrick, district music supervisor, conducted weekly singing assemblies. The precocious Alfred Lee Booth, Class of 1911, directed an orchestra, organized a boys' glee club, and composed the school's alma mater in 1910. The new physical training classes in 1914 practiced movement and dance. Liturgical music paved the way for high school choral work. Dramatics clubs thrived in each year's senior, junior, and sophomore classes. Yet the Webster Groves School District's hiring of a stellar arts faculty in the late 1920s and early 1930s focused attention on music, drama, and the visual arts, making these disciplines an integral part of the high school curriculum.

HANS J. LEMCKE

Born in Germany, Hans Lemcke began his musical training at age six, first on the violin, then the piano, and later the trumpet. At age fourteen, he began composing light marches for orchestras and bands. His father, Henry Lemcke, led the German Marine Band and directed the massed bands at the St. Louis World's Fair in 1904. Young Hans Lemcke loved the United States and returned to play professionally in bands and to complete his music degree at Illinois Wesleyan in Bloomington.

When Mr. Lemcke arrived at Webster Groves High School in 1926, he was already a noted composer of music for the piano, voice, orchestras, and military bands, including the United States Navy Band. He also possessed a working knowledge of all band and orchestral instruments. At Webster Groves High School, he assisted Mr. W. B. Heyne in establishing a music department.

Mr. Lemcke found the fledgling senior and junior high band in disarray, so he began with organization, instrumentation, and constant practice. Since there were no music rooms, the band practiced in the old Armory or wherever they could find an empty room. Yet when state competitions at Columbia, Missouri, rolled around in the spring, the band had improved enough to win third place.

The band grew steadily in size and sophistication under Mr. Lemcke's leadership and eventually earned national recognition. His duties included the concert band, orchestra and string orchestra,

The Webster fight song is an adaptation of "On Wisconsin," while the Alma Mater was written by Alfred Lee Booth, a student at the high school, in 1910.

facing page: The 1940 stage crew prepares to raise the curtain on opening night.

23

Hans Lemcke took a co-curricular band, and in a few short years developed a K–12 instrumental music program that sought to offer every student the opportunity to learn to play an instrument.

chamber music group, small ensembles, and the marching band. He became school district music supervisor in 1931.

Since Mr. Lemcke believed that every student should have a chance to play an instrument, he promoted a "start them early" music philosophy. Beginning with fourth graders, he administered a music aptitude test to match high scorers with instruments and to recommend private lessons with professional musicians. Yet he did not discourage low scorers from taking lessons and playing in the band. Reportedly one in every three students played an instrument, and by the time instrumental music students reached junior high, they were ready to play in a full-scale band.

Perhaps the most celebrated event of Mr. Lemcke's career occurred in 1927, when the "March King" John Philip Sousa, directed the Webster Groves High School Band. The Sousa-Lemcke connection began in 1900, when Sousa visited Lemcke's father's naval band in Germany during a world tour. In 1923, Hans played coronet in Sousa's band for four months. So when Sousa came to St. Louis for a series of concerts at the old Loew's State Theater, Hans attended the performance and met backstage with Sousa, who promised to visit Webster Groves High School.

The special assembly was set for Monday morning, on November 21, 1927. Sousa examined the organization of the school's music program and led the band in playing his "Stars and Stripes Forever." Decades later, in a September 26, 1968, *St. Louis Post-Dispatch* interview, Mr. Lemcke, recalled Sousa's visit:

Mr. Lemcke invited his friend John Philip Sousa to the high school on November 21, 1927, to direct the Statesmen band in a special assembly for the student body.

Our band was still in its infancy. I remember Sousa trying to evoke some "accents" from the band, but they would not come. The band did not respond to his wishes. I was standing behind the scenes and looked at Mr. Sousa and smiled, and he smiled back at me, and went on and finished the march, with much applause.

Mr. Lemcke's attempts to "evoke accents" from his band and orchestra students remained as important as his search for talent. He called music "the humanities of life," adding, "I wonder whether the schools haven't forgotten to teach in their curriculums the things that are good for the soul—the things that everybody lives with everyday: an appreciation of nature, the trees; of rhythms."

Mr. Lemcke composed "March, Webster High," a "rhythmic military piece," to coincide with the dedication of the new high school building in 1927. The theme of the selection is the melody of the school's alma mater and can be played both as a piano solo and for band and orchestra. His son, Henry J. Lemcke, followed in his father's footsteps as Webster Groves High School band director. Hans Lemcke taught and supervised music programs in Webster Groves for thirty-seven years. Before his retirement, he left this postscript:

A student who has finished our course of instrumental instruction finds himself equipped to continue his study at college and adopt music as his life work. Some of our young people have gone from our department to various colleges to major in music. They are definitely preparing themselves for careers in the music world.

Miss "Rep"

"Eyes . . . eyes. . . ." To say that Esther Replogle "ably directed" the Girls Glee Club, the Boys Glee Club, the A Cappella Choir, the Mixed Chorus, and the high school's first operetta is already an understatement. The diminutive director in stocking feet drew the music into her being, recycled it into her students, and extracted it with surgical precision. She was artist and purist, consumed by music, and born for the stage.

Once the concert was completed, "Queen Esther" has time to relax with her singers.

The annual Vespers Service was a December tradition that grew in popularity to necessitate multiple performances.

Miss Rep prepares her choir for one of their many radio guest performances on KMOX.

Miss "Rep," as she was called by her students, came to Webster Groves High School in 1928. She taught forty-one years in Webster Groves before retiring in 1968. She grew up in Carthage, Missouri, a town claiming Belle Starr as its most famous woman outlaw and Carthage itself as "Queen City of the South West." She majored in mathematics at Stephens College in Columbia, Missouri, a college with a history of educating strong-willed women with a penchant for innovative leadership. After transferring from Stephens to University of Missouri, Miss Replogle graduated with a vocal music degree and taught in Carthage before joining the faculty at Webster Groves High School.

A martinet when it came to discipline, she was free-spirited with the song, the sacred and patriotic bordering on ecstasy. . . . And of course they loved her—choir students considered her more friend than teacher, parents extolled her standing-room-only performances, administrators rewarded her undeniable service, and the community basked in her fame.

As groundbreaking as she was spectacular, she directed the school's first light operetta, *Sylvia*, in the spring of 1928. Set in the eighteenth century, the two-act musical portrays the dilemma of two girls, an English lady of the court and a farm girl, who exchange places yet discover they prefer their original stations. The performance featured sixty-four cast members and twenty-nine orchestra students, beginning a tradition of collaboration among music, art, and drama faculty still thriving as the "fall musical."

The music department appeared at numerous community events each year, such as this concert at the Moolah Temple.

Miss Rep favored a cappella work. She believed that accompaniment masked errors in sight-reading, and she insisted that her students master the notes. Only the most talented Glee Club seniors sang in the a cappella choir. Practices were Monday nights and Wednesdays before school until 1933, when it became part of the curriculum.

The Music Department had its own space by 1935. Vocal and choral rooms were located on the first floor in the south wing of the building. The band room was on the second floor, and sound-proof practice rooms were located on the third floor above the Little Theater. High school choirs performed at the Missouri State Teachers Convention, at Washington University's Interstate Music Contest, at the University of Missouri Interscholastic Meet, at the National Music Association's Convention in Oklahoma City, and at the Webster Groves High School baccalaureate service and commencement exercises.

The pinnacle of the year came a week before Christmas with the annual candlelight vespers service when lines blurred between church and state, when the school auditorium was transformed into a mock cathedral, and when capacity audiences required two, three, and finally five performances to showcase the Nativity and mass choirs in full splendor. What had begun as a simple Christmas pageant in December 1933 grew into an elaborate ceremony.

The first year, the Boys Glee Club walked down the auditorium aisles with lighted candles. The second year program added a symphony orchestra, and a cappella alumni returned to participate.

Eugene "Woody" Woods was drama teacher, producer, and director, as well as the designer of Webster's Little Theater.

In the play *The Petrified Forest*, convict and waitress discuss life in a materialistic society.

The third year featured "Why the Chimes Rang," a semi-operetta. During the program, Miss Rep explained that her inspiration came from a book she read about a tradition in France portraying the first Christmas, and she wanted to recreate a program similar to the Nativity celebrations in European cathedrals.

Superintendent Willard E. Goslin encouraged the program to establish a memorable school tradition. Billed as a "religious service," the program was challenged in future decades, but as late as the mid-1960s, Miss Rep, who directed five choirs at the First Congregational Church and sat on the board of the St. Louis Christmas Carol Association in addition to her teaching duties, considered the school program a cultural tradition and a service to the community.

She was recognized for her community service in 1964, when she was selected as one of ten *St. Louis Globe-Democrat* "Women of the Year" for her work in the field of fine arts. Also, like Hans Lemcke, she was declared Webster Groves Chamber of Commerce Citizen of the Year—Mr. Lemcke in 1959 and Esther Replogle in 1967. She was often quoted as saying that she would rather be a choir director at Webster Groves High School than the Queen of England. For forty years, Her Majesty, the Queen of Vocal Music, enjoyed the fame and privileges of both positions.

"Woody"

The high school's Little Theater opened with its first play, *Little Ol' Boy*, on April 15, 1935. The theater itself was modeled after Yale University's Little Theater, and the play, billed as a "vivid yet pathetic story of reformatory life," required actors to wear uniforms from Missouri's Booneville School for Boys. In short, it was a typical "Woody" production: realistic, tense, and provocative while requiring near-professional-level acting.

A native of Bowling Green, a small town in central Missouri, Eugene Wood began his acting career with leading roles at Kirksville State Teachers College in northeast Missouri. After transferring to Colorado Teachers College, he continued to act in leading roles and earned a degree in dramatics. He performed in summer stock companies in the Theatre in the Woods in Boothbay, Maine; in the Berkshire Playhouse in Massachusetts; and in the Globe Theatre in San Diego.

When Wood came to Webster Groves High School in 1929, he taught dramatics and speech in the ninth grade, but when senior high dramatics teacher Dorothy Stanley resigned, he moved to the high school the following year. Under Wood's direction, the Drama Department resembled stock theater or a theater guild, with production after production, one play in performance and another in rehearsal.

Wood's production staffs learned and assumed responsibility for every phase of the theater: lighting, makeup, costumes, set design, stage and property management, business and advertising, house management, and directing. He developed an ensemble cast of serious, hardworking actors, and he amassed a following of avid theatergoers, apparent in the eagerly awaited performances and capacity audiences.

The first year, 1930, Mr. Wood began with seven one-act plays. The next year, he produced four longer plays, along with shorter ones. He increased the number to five major productions in 1933 and six in 1934. In 1940, he produced seven major plays. All together he directed sixty plays during his eleven years at Webster Groves High School.

"Woody," as his students called him, offered experimental theater in a naturalistic setting. Whether serious plays or comedies, classic Shakespeare or contemporary drama, he rarely retreated from political or social commentary—or from "adult" material. His plays were "cutting edge," often the newest works of rising playwrights.

His "peace propaganda play" production, *Spread Eagle*, published by journalists-playwrights George S. Brooks and Walter Lister and dealing with the United States' intervention into Mexico, had been a hit on Broadway in 1927. His 1938 production of *The Petrified Forest*, published a year

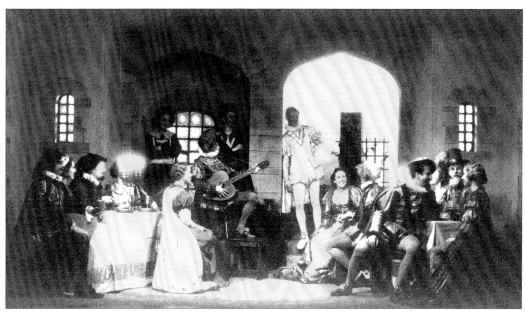

Produced in 1936, *The Taming of the Shrew* was an elaborately staged period piece.

earlier by Robert Sherwood, portrayed a young intellectual pitted against an escaped convict while provoking questions about the value of life in a materialistic society. Other productions spanning Wood's prolific career at high school include *Holiday, Stage Door, Journey's End, The Ghost of Yankee Doodle, What a Life, Richard II, As You Like It, The Taming of the Shrew, Comedy of Errors, Twelfth Night,* and *Our Town*—his last Webster Groves High School production.

Thornton Wilder's *Our Town*, which had its world premiere in 1938, proved a fitting finale for Woody and Webster Groves. Set in Grover's Corner, a small New Hampshire town in the early 1900s, the play uses no scenery and few props, forcing the audience to focus on character. The Stage Manager serves as commentator for Emily Webb, who died in childbirth and now fulfills her wish of reliving the day of her twelfth birthday by conversing with other dead family members and residents. Sadly, she knows their future and her own. More importantly, she discovers the need to embrace life's daily pleasures. Grover's Corner was Woody's parting gift to Webster Groves.

When Eugene Wood left Webster Groves High School in 1940, he was regarded as one of the best high school dramatics teachers in the country. He accepted a teaching position at the Clifford J. Scott High School in East Orange, New Jersey, because of its proximity to New York City theater circles and because it gave him the opportunity to study makeup, voice, and stage design at the Chekhov School. Also, he wanted to maintain contacts with his friends in summer stock companies. At Webster Groves High School, he left a Little Theater that he designed and a theater tradition with a reputation for sophisticated and unconventional drama.

Pete Myers formed the Regimental Band, Webster's first marching band.

"PETE" MYERS

His name was Edwin D. Myers, but students and colleagues called him "Pete." He actually preferred "Ah-pe-pe-tah," meaning "White Eagle," an honorary name that the Blackfoot Indian tribe gave him in 1942. As a teacher he was the quiet force behind two high school departments—art and music. During summer retreats, he was Indian chief.

Pete Myers came to Webster Groves High School in 1933 with a degree in art from Northeast Missouri State Teachers College in Kirksville. Both practical and innovative, he served as the school's artist in residence for thirty-one years.

Pete Myers, "artist in residence," spent his summers as director in Indian lore at Culver Military Academy's Woodcraft Camp.

In 1935, when the Art Department moved from two crowded rooms for its two art teachers, Mr. Myers and Miss Sebee Rowley, to large, connected classrooms with an office and storeroom, the high school's Studio Art Department began to blossom. Pete taught one advanced art class and four beginning classes.

More mentor than teacher, "He instructed, but he never dictated," one student told an *Echo* reporter after Pete Myer's death in 1963. His students produced school posters, stage designs, murals, and lettering for cards and books while mastering the techniques of drawing and painting.

They gathered informally in his classroom while he sat meditatively in his office. His room was covered with stacks of paintings, sketches, letters, and notebooks. Yet proof of student learning lay in the art prizes his students won in local and state competitions.

It is unclear whether Pete Myers was an artist who became a musician or a musician who became an artist. He organized the high school's Regimental Band, precursor to the marching band in 1937, with the support of Mr. Hans Lemcke. He volunteered to help with scenery for school musicals and to make decorations for special occasions throughout the school and the district. He even sponsored a student Model Railroad Club.

Signs of the teacher and the man lay in his desk drawer filled with collages, paints, brushes, charcoal, pencils . . . and a cigar. As "White Eagle," his spirit hovered near Culver, Indiana, off the shores of Lake Maxinkuchee, where for thirty summers Pete Myers served as director of Indian lore and the Drum and Bugle Corps. Here, he wrote his own script, produced twenty-one plays for fireside gatherings, painted his face and those of his actors, then danced to the music of his own drum.

MR. HIXSON'S FAREWELL

When James T. Hixson resigned as principal in 1943, the blueprint for Webster Groves High School was complete. What had begun as a two-story schoolhouse in 1907 was a sprawling high school with

The students pay tribute to Mr. Hixson at his retirement as principal of WGHS in 1943.

nearly 2,000 students. The addition of elective courses in business and the arts expanded options for students preparing for college or planning a vocation. Extracurricular activities and athletics kept students involved and motivated. Community commitment and support, evident in a succession of bond issue campaigns, assured maintenance of the district's central high school.

Out of the spotlight, Mr. Hixson remained a private man and an old-fashioned leader. Cultivating the intellect and character, he insisted, was the primary aim of education. Against the rumbles of world war, he reflected on his thirty-six years of service—the building years of the first decade, the glory years of the twenties, the sobering years of the thirties, and now the uncertain years of the forties.

No doubt the future would be kind to Webster Groves High School, as the past had been kind to him—the gentle patriarch, a little grayer, more subdued, but always wise. The 1944 *Echo* yearbook honored him with this tribute:

> *We know of no other person who has given so much service in our school as Mr. Hixson. His strong Christian character and spirit and his high standard of scholarship have exerted an enduring and far-reaching influence. His keen sense of humor, firm but reasonable discipline, genuine interest in each individual student as well as in every activity and problem of our school—all of these qualities have made Mr. Hixson a symbol of the spirit of Webster Groves High School.*

Part II

TRANSITION

Chapter 4

> *"America offers to every boy and girl, rich or poor, the opportunity to obtain an education. Education is the heritage of American youth. There is no richer patrimony. It is not merely a precious boon, it is a patriotic duty. None is so poor, nor is any so rich that he may not enter into his national heritage."*
>
> —From the foreword to the 1933 Douglass yearbook

In North Webster, Douglass High School was also making history. In an era when segregation was legal and dual school systems for blacks and whites were the norm, Douglass High School in 1925 became the only African American high school in St. Louis County, as well as the first, in 1932, to be accredited by the state and to gain membership in the prestigious North Central Association of Colleges and Secondary Schools.

From the beginning, public education in Webster Groves was as much a moral commitment as a legal arrangement, owing to the pioneering role of four churches: First Congregational Church, Webster Groves Presbyterian Church, Emmanuel Episcopal Church, and First Baptist Church—all established in 1866. First Baptist Church became the site of black schooling in 1866, when Mrs. Dotswell, a white woman, volunteered to teach the first class of black children.

Douglass elementary students enjoy the outdoors.

In 1868, the newly organized Webster Groves School District assumed responsibility for educating black and white children. A district census revealed a potential school population of 225 white children and 30 black children between the ages of five and twenty-one. Miss Emma Babcock, a white woman, began teaching the black students in September 1869 while charging thirty dollars for transportation expenses as the only compensation. In October 1869, Mr. T. L. Slocum, at a salary of $1,400 a year, and Miss Augusta Murfelt, at a salary of $500, began teaching the white children at the First Congregational Church.

In 1870, the School Board appointed Mr. T. A. Busch, the district's first black teacher, to teach a class of twenty-three black students at First Baptist Church. Thirteen black students from the Rock Hill School District enrolled on a tuition basis of $100 a year. Classes met nine months a year and closed for harvest seasons, and the county, state, or both contributed funding as required by early state statutes for the support of public education.

In 1872, the School Board rented a one-room building on a lot west of First Baptist for ten dollars a month and purchased the building and the lot the following year, making this the first district

facing page: The Douglass High School majorettes show off their new uniforms.

Douglass High, which opened in 1925, was more than a school. It was the focal point for the African American community for education, interaction, and activities.

school purchased for black students in Webster Groves. Teachers between 1872 and 1890 were Mrs. Swayner, Mr. Masterly, Mr. Perry Momatt, Mr. Needle, Mr. Mitchell, Mr. Morris, Mr. Johnson, Mrs. Clancey, and Mrs. Jennie Davis.

Early in 1890, the one-room school burned to the ground and classes moved back to First Baptist Church, then to an old store on Gore and Moody. In 1892, the school district built a new two-room frame school on Holland Avenue between Fox and Ravine. The district hired a new principal, Mr. Agee, one teacher, and one aide. Mrs. Lulu Farmer taught the older students while an assistant taught the younger children. School enrollment was approximately ninety students.

In 1895, a group of black leaders proposed that the School Board name the school the "Frederick Douglass School," after the famous ex-slave, orator, journalist, and abolitionist. The board agreed, and Mrs. Lulu Farmer was appointed principal.

In 1898, the Douglass School held its first eighth-grade graduation for three students: Arnold Brown, Mary Brown, and Theodore Morrison. Yet since there was no high school available for black students in Webster Groves, students continuing their education had to enroll at Sumner High School in St. Louis City on a tuition basis. In 1902, the first seven students from North Webster took the train to Union Station and walked three blocks to Charles Sumner High School, at that time located at 11th and Spruce streets. Sumner, founded in 1875, prided itself on being the oldest African American high school west of the Mississippi River.

Meanwhile at Douglass, two principals set the pattern of schooling during the early twentieth century. Lincoln Nelson, in 1903, initiated school and community improvement clubs and arranged for weekly speakers and discussion of books borrowed from the Congregational Church's reading room. Professor Thomas A. Moore, a stern and proper man, from 1904 to 1925 taught eighth grade mathematics to Douglass students and established the school's rigorous academic and martial order.

Still, demands for an African American high school in Webster Groves continued. Students commuting to Sumner faced overcrowding. Black parents earning as little as fifty cents a day found it difficult to pay the $100 tuition. Further, when Douglass's enrollment reached 108 students in 1915, North Webster parents appealed to the School Board to provide high school education for their children. They pointed out that Webster Groves High School had opened on Selma Avenue in

1907 for white students, but eight years later, there was no high school for the district's black students.

Exhausted by unsuccessful appeals to the School Board, a group of parents organized to seek legal remedy. In 1917, Frank Stone and Augustus Ewing from Webster Groves and Mr. and Mrs. William H. Jenkins from Kirkwood hired a lawyer to take their case to Jefferson City on behalf of their children and black students throughout the state. In 1918, the Missouri Supreme Court upheld public school segregation yet required districts to provide "equal education" for black and white students, in compliance with federal law, ensuing from the 1896 U.S. Supreme Court decision in *Plessy v. Ferguson*. The Webster Groves School Board paid $75 of the $100 tuition for black district students to attend Sumner High School before deciding to establish a "High School Department" at Douglass in 1925.

Mr. Herbert S. Davis, Douglass's first high school principal, oversaw the transition,

The Douglass Faculty in 1920
Mrs. Edith Retter, Nellie Salmon,
Prin. T. A. Moore, Mrs. Susie Lewis
H. J. Simms. Mrs. Marg. Parker

T. A. Moore (right, back row), principal of Douglass, gathers his faculty for this 1920 photo.

starting with the ninth grade and phasing in one grade each year, to complete a full high school program by 1928. Mr. Davis, holding a master's degree from the University of Illinois, strove from 1925 to 1928 to assemble a high school faculty and to establish an academic program, athletic teams, and clubs and organizations on a par with Sumner and the best white high schools in the region.

He was allotted books from Webster Groves High School but denied permission to use the gymnasium and auditorium. So he created a gymnasium in a dance hall behind Summytt's Drug Store. (Before World War I through the Depression, the pharmacist Elvis Summytt and his wife Lee Etta operated the only black drugstore in Webster Groves.) Davis promoted school clubs in speech and drama to prepare for state competitions. He worked with the Douglass PTA to raise money for band equipment, gym uniforms, school dances, and other extracurricular activities. He started a summer school in 1928.

Douglass High School held its first commencement in May 1929 for nine graduates: Hildered Campbell, Mattye Gill, Louis Harden, David Hawkins, Mayda Morgan, Helen Morton, Imelda Thomas, Robert Thomas, and Thelma Weeks. Mr. Davis too was leaving. He had accepted a social studies teaching position at the new Vashon High School in St. Louis. Mr. Howell Berkeley Goins,

Principal Herbert Davis, bottom center, is surrounded by Douglass's first graduating class.

Douglass High School's social studies teacher since 1926, became the high school's last and longest-tenured principal, serving from 1929 to 1956.

H. B. Goins was to Douglass High School what J. T. Hixson was to Webster Groves High School. Both men came from upstate Missouri, Hixson from Marshall and Goins from Louisiana, Missouri, where he attended Lincoln High School. Both men quietly inserted themselves into the community and quietly became institutions within their respective schools. Each was intent on making his high school "tops in the county." Goins, however, assumed responsibility for elementary through senior high school and for nonresident students from more than ten different municipalities.

The son of a doctor, "Professor Goins," as Douglass parents and students called him, attended Sedalia, Missouri's George R. Smith College, a small black college operating from 1894 to 1925 under the auspices of the Methodist Episcopal Church and later merging with Philander Smith College in Little Rock, Arkansas. (George R. Smith College claimed the composer Scott Joplin, "King of Ragtime," as its most famous alumnus.) Goins also completed undergraduate work at Illinois State Normal University and graduate work at the State University of Iowa. Before coming to Webster Groves, he served as principal for five years at the Dunbar School in Elsberry, Missouri.

Mr. Goins was also an early leader in regional and state education. He served as president of the St. Louis County Association of Negro Teachers and as a contributing editor to the *State Journal of Education*, the publication of the Missouri State Association of Negro Teachers.

When Mr. Goins came to Douglass High School in 1926, he joined a talented faculty in an era when "the cream of the crop" black teachers taught in black schools and black colleges. John Palmer came from Lincoln University and taught mathematics and geography. Ruth Dixon studied at the University of Nebraska and taught English. Conrad L. Thomas came from the University of Kansas and taught biology, physics, and chemistry. Alice Armstrong also attended the University of Kansas and taught art. Helen Goins came from Lincoln University to teach physical education and music. Edna Hill attended Wilberforce University in Ohio and taught home economics. P. K. "Kenneth" Boulding came from Geneva College in Pennsylvania and taught social science. Marguerite Smith studied at Wilberforce University and taught French and Latin. Cyrus B. Taylor came from Hampton Institute in Virginia and taught manual training and physical education.

Professor Goins ran a "tight ship" for faculty and students alike. His religious college training accustomed him to a moral regimen, and he insisted that his teachers conduct themselves strictly as role models. Women teachers were discouraged from marrying. All teachers were discouraged from frequenting local nightclubs, and they were urged to reside in North Webster. They could rent a room from Annie Polk.

Misbehaving students served after-school detention. Miscreants and serious offenders were expelled. Discipline was reinforced by parents. Punishment at school meant punishment at home. Busy parents trusted the word of the principal and teacher over the hushed protests of their children.

"Today's pupils are tomorrow's voting citizens," Professor Goins told his students. Douglass's aim was to train "good leaders" and "good followers." He also believed that the school must be unified with, as well as represent, the community. The "Douglass Pride" manifested itself in decorum—distinction in academics, status in club membership, poise in the choir and orchestra, composure on the athletic field, suaveness on the dance floor, and pageantry on graduation day. Douglass High School became that school on "the Hill" celebrating its community spirit, prominent extended families, and social grace with utmost dignity.

H. B. Goins instilled "Douglass pride" in his students for thirty-eight years.

In the 1930s and '40s, African American students seeking a high school education in the St. Louis region had three choices: Sumner, Douglass, or Vashon. Home districts of nonresident students paid their tuition, but commuting students furnished their own transportation. At Douglass, students came from as near as Kirkwood, Richmond Heights, Brentwood, and Ladue and from as far as Kinloch, Berkeley, Ferguson, Florissant, Bridgeton, Manchester, Chesterfield, Valley Park, Glencoe, Pacific, and Washington, Missouri. Many took the Kirkwood-Ferguson streetcar, Missouri Pacific train, or organized carpools. Some rented rooms from North Webster families or worked for white families in exchange for room and board. Families moved from outstate to North Webster so their children could get a "good education."

Despite the Depression, the 1930s brought a period of expansion. Basement rooms had been added in 1913, and three rooms were added for the High School Department beginning in 1925. The Webster Groves School Board lauded these improvements as "the best investment in social betterment the district has ever made," while relying on a combination of bond issue money and federal funding for Douglass renovations. In 1931, a gymnasium, office, and typing room were added. A 1933 bond issue, together with loans and grants from the Federal Emergency Administration of Public Works, allowed for improvement, addition, and completion of the cafeteria, kindergarten, and library, as well as for the purchase of industrial arts and home economics equipment. A 1933 grant from the Federal Emergency Fund for Education funded a night school, a popular program for teenagers and adults working during the school day.

A premier faculty, the 1933 teachers at Douglass were (top row, left to right) John Palmer, Ruth Dixon, C. L. Thomas; (center, left to right) Alice Armstrong, Helen Goins, Edna Hill; (bottom, left to right) P. K. Boulding, Marguerite Smith, Cyrus Taylor.

Herbert Davis's dreams of a preeminent black high school were taking shape with Professor Goins's urgings of a strict diet of homework and high expectations. Courses included English, Latin, French, Spanish, mathematics, physical education, social studies, geography, biology, physics, chemistry, manual arts training, home economics, art, and music.

Emphasis was placed on vocational education, particularly in business courses. Former Douglass teacher Mrs. Melzetta Brown explained that her courses in business English, secretarial practice, shorthand, and typing prepared students for skills they would use immediately after graduation. "The courses were so complete that they could go right out and get a job without any further training. That's the way we had to train them, because at the time, we still had the separate educational set-up, and it was necessary for the students to learn something that they could use later on."

With an emphasis on academics, Douglass's curriculum contained laboratory courses such as this 1950s chemistry class.

Douglass School was already a force in the music world. As early as the 1920s, Harvey J. Simms, a Douglass elementary teacher, together with visiting instructor P. B. Lankford, formed the first Douglass Band, whose members Joe Thomas and Buddy Reese became professional musicians years later. Douglass High School eventually boasted a fifty- to sixty-piece band. There was also a school orchestra and a high school choir of fifty students directed by Mr. Earl Eulingbourgh from 1935 to 1940.

Walter Lathen and Kenneth Billups took the music program into a new era, with the support and cooperation of Hans Lemcke, instrumental music director at Webster Groves High School and district music supervisor beginning in 1931. Mr. Lemcke's philosophy of making instrumental training available to every child not only encouraged band participation but also led to the search for outstanding music directors. Lathen and Billups were more than capable.

Reportedly, Professor Goins and Hans Lemcke recruited Walter Lathen from Cairo, Illinois, to direct the Music Department at Douglass High School. Students took music lessons after school and rehearsed in the band at night. Lathen developed a fifty-piece band, won honors at music festivals, and conducted the first African American high school band to play before the Suburban Music Educators Association.

Kenneth Billups, from 1943 to 1949, became a legend at Douglass and garnered a higher status after leaving Douglass when he became head of Sumner's Music Department and choral director of the St. Louis Symphony. At Sumner, the accomplished director, arranger, and composer trained the internationally renowned Legend Singers and the opera singer Grace Bumbry. A graduate of Lincoln University in Jefferson City, Missouri, Billups's legacy at Douglass High School was the school's alma mater, "Hail to Douglass," which he composed in 1943.

North Webster was extended family to its residents, and Douglass High School functioned as its center, becoming a crossroads of community events and after-school clubs and organizations. As early as the 1930s, students joined the English Honor Club, Glee Club, Orchestra, Student Self-Government Association, *Oracle* yearbook staff, Junior Red Cross, Hi-Y (high school division of the North Webster YMCA), and Girl Reserves, service club counterpart to the boys' Hi-Y. Later, the Etiquette Club and *Entre Nous* emphasized manners. Other organizations included the Drama Club, Home Economics Club, Human Relations Club, Teenage Book Club, Leaders' Club, tennis club, and National Honor Society—collectively encompassing a range of personal, social, and academic interests and distinctions.

Walter Ambrose, Class of 1937, in the 1979 edition of Webster Groves High School's *In Retrospect*, recalled the array of extracurricular and athletic activities at Douglass:

> *We had math club, a foreign language club. . . . We had a complete student council. We only had major athletic activities. We had football, basketball, and track. We had a dynamite girls' softball team, but no boys. I thought it was a well-rounded program. We got a lot of participation because of the number of students.*

The Douglass band, under the direction of Walther Lathen, presented concerts, participated in state music contests, and performed at community events.

Douglass had between 230 and 250 students in the late 1930s. By the late 1940s, there were 600 students enrolled in kindergarten through high school.

In athletics, Mrs. Helen Goins coached the girls' basketball team, which played Booneville, alumni, YWCA, Argus, Alton, Festus, and Desoto. The "Argus Girls," known as the "St. Louis Champions," were both rivals and idols whom the girls rarely defeated. The boys' basketball team played in the Illinois-Missouri League as well as in Columbia and Hannibal. Closer to home, they played Sumner, Vashon, and Washington Technical High School (in St. Louis). In Illinois, they played Lincoln High School, Lovejoy, and Edwardsville.

The boys' winning season began with the arrival of Coach Cyrus Taylor. Before, the football squad, coached by Mr. Kenneth Boulding, scored well in practice but succumbed to formidable Sumner and Vashon teams in the early 1930s. Their fortunes changed when Mr. William Bell later coached winning football, basketball, and track teams.

Teen town was a time for dancing, conversation, and refreshments.

Nineteen forty-five was a watershed year for Douglass. District voters passed a bond issue to build a new Douglass elementary school, allowing for more space at the junior high and senior high, and the Douglass High School football team became Missouri State Champions. For years, students and staff endured cramped quarters, resulting in portable rooms on the playground, and for years PTA President Walter Rusan pressed the Webster Groves School Board for a new building. The existing building, Douglass parents argued, dated back to 1892, and elementary, junior high, and senior high students used the same antiquated facilities. District administrators offered sympathy but no school. Money, they said, was unavailable.

The 1945 bond issue allowed for the purchase of land and the construction of a new elementary

Douglass offered football, basketball, baseball, and track to its male athletes.

The girls basketball team finished the 1933 season with a record of 8–2, losing to Alton and St. Louis Argus.

school. The land extended from Holland to North Elm and from Fox Place to Ravine. Dedicated on October 19, 1947, Douglass Elementary School contained thirteen classrooms, a gymnasium, cafeteria, kindergarten, shop, and playroom.

Douglass High School and Webster Groves High School in the 1950s operated in separate spheres, but the law would have its day when the U.S. Supreme Court, in Brown v. the Board of Education of Topeka, Kansas, outlawed public school segregation. Racial segregation, the Court added, was inherently unequal, detrimental, and unconstitutional. Local response was immediate. Douglass Elementary School, enrolling 294 students in kindergarten through sixth grade, remained open, with Mr. Goins remaining as principal. Douglass High School, enrolling 412 students in grades 7 through 12, closed its doors. The 189 nonresident students at Douglass High School returned to their home school districts.

In August 1954, Dr. Leonard A. Steger, superintendent of the Webster Groves School District from 1944 to 1956, announced the district's four-step program of school integration:

1. Integration in the adult evening school has been accomplished.

2. Integration in the Webster Groves–Kirkwood Summer School will become effective June 1955.

3. The integrated elementary school program will become effective September 1955.

4. The secondary program of integration will be effected September 1956.

For the time being, the 1954–55 school year operated as usual while awaiting "fully explicit" announcements when the Supreme Court reconvened in October 1954.

Graduation Day (date unknown) brings classmates together for their final high school celebration.

The Webster Groves School District's delay to integrate Webster Groves High School followed with this explanation in September 1955: "It was thought that by postponing integration at the secondary school level there would be time to develop both staff and community understanding. Also some pupils outside the Webster Groves District may wish to continue as pupils in the Douglass High School through the school year 1955–56."

School integration at Webster Groves High School was set for the fall of 1956. The law had settled the injustice if not the iniquity. Douglass High School all-stars would have to find their place in a new school where the seats were already assigned, a school with its own champions backed by a fifty-year-old tradition. Left behind were the teachers who knew them, the community that cheered them, and a high school beneath the rubble with a phantom song, "Hail to Thee Douglass, Dear old school . . . rang through the halls and over the hills. Purple and gold fight on."

Chapter 5

> *"Every class is unique. Every class makes a distinct contribution to the life, leadership, and history of a school. For each member of a class, may the years invested here be an introduction and a challenge to greater opportunities and to a rewarding life."*
> —Howard A. Latta, 1955

In the fall of 1943, Webster Groves High School welcomed an "old friend and a new principal." For thirteen years Mr. Howard A. Latta served as an assistant principal in charge of the junior high, and following Mr. Hixson's retirement, Mr. Latta was the natural choice for uncertain times.

Mr. Latta was the link between old and new: reassuring youth in a world at war, steering the high school through "growing pains" of the 1950s, and shielding students against the social upheaval of the 1960s. When he retired in 1968, he had endured mounting enrollment, mandated school integration, junior-high boundary disputes, national media exposure controversy, staff increases and turnovers, and the beginnings of student unrest.

Yet it was not all rough sailing. In 1944, the new superintendent, Dr. Leonard A. Steger, moved into the new central office administration building at 16 Selma Avenue, creating more space for Mr. Latta and his associate principal, Dr. Joe Verby, director of guidance and counseling. The magnificent new $400,000 Roberts Gymnasium, in honor of the late Charlie Roberts, was dedicated in 1947. The successful Rock Hill School District annexation in 1948 increased the student population and district revenues.

Athletic teams rallied around a new generation of coaches. The district completed Memorial Field on the once-disputed "Forty Acres." The high school bands and orchestras under Hans Lemcke and choirs under Esther Replogle took first prize at Washington University music competitions. Christmas Vespers services grew larger. The Little Theater debuted play after play. School clubs and organizations subsided and reinvented themselves. Mr. Latta stayed the course.

He had grown up in Winfield, Kansas, a small town in the south-central part of the state, and completed undergraduate work in social science at Kansas State Teachers College in Pittsburg. He completed graduate work at the University of Missouri in Columbia, Columbia University in New York City, and Washington University in St. Louis.

Mr. Latta worked to provide a climate that maximized learning.

facing page: The cheerleaders encourage the crowd to support the Statesmen as they take on Southwest High.

45

Together again on the steps of Webster High where they once congregated in spare moments are Webster alumni Jack Clayton, Bob Collins, Ed Borman, Baird Sick and Ed Busch.

Before coming to Webster Groves in 1931, Mr. Latta served as principal of a high school of 200 students in Cedar Vale, Kansas. In Webster Groves, he headed the junior high while teaching a ninth-grade class in algebra.

A year earlier, in 1930, Mr. Hixson had been appointed district director of research, and Mr. George A. F. Hay became the new principal of Webster Groves High School. When Mr. Hay resigned after one year, Mr. Hixson returned as high school principal, and Mr. Latta was hired as assistant principal for the 1931–32 school year.

Like Mr. Hixson, Mr. Latta supported a solid academic curriculum, but he agreed with former Superintendent Willard E. Goslin that the high school of the future must also prepare the student entering a trade or vocation. Webster Groves High School would not only become the "people's college" but the "people's high school" as well.

Mr. Latta's first duty was to comfort the living. Charles E. Garner, the district's superintendent of research, published the following results of a 1944 district "social participation" survey titled

"What Is Right with the Youth of Webster Groves":

It appears that youth are reasonably busy, happy people. They are grouped in families with enough activity to keep most of them engaged at least five evenings a week. They read, listen to the radio, or go to the show once a week, and most of them get home as quickly as the parents could.

We believe parents sincere and youth wholesome. We believe that war prospects make boys restless and home tense at times, but most of all we believe there is nothing inherently wrong with the youth that patience and guidance can not cure.

So Webster Groves teenagers were "normal."

Mr. Latta's second obligation was to honor the dead. In a memorial service on May 27, 1947, he called the roll of sixty-one Webster Groves High School alumni lost to war:

These 1962 candidates for Miss Webster enjoy Memorial Pool before the Fourth of July activities.

J. Glenn Anderson	Milton Held	Raymond Mutrux
Barney H. Biederman	William Hobbs	Allan Payne
George Bohn	William K. Holaday	Wesley Niles Perkins
William Brown	Robert Jack Holt	Walter L. Pfeffer, Jr.
William Buck	Charles Horr	Larry Reynolds
Thomas Cole	Elwood Jones	W. Clark Schmidt
Robert B. Combs	Richard King Kaufman	Robert Schwabe, II
James Cook	Walter Kaufman	Thomas Henry Sears
James W. Corner	Norbert Leo Lamm	Williams M. Sherrill
Robert S. Donald	Douglas Tyler Leeper	Jr. Robert Foss Shipley
Robert E. Field	Robert L. Linss	Josephine M. Smith
John Lloyd Fillo	Daniel Bader Martin	James W. Stevenson
Harold D. Fitzgerald	Richard McKibben	Robert B. Thompson
Robert Sanford Gaston	Gerard Mason	James Townsend
James A. Gentles	Martin Meili	Robert Van Benthuysen
C. Gingam Goerner	Theodore H. Meyer	Alfred Jean Whitehorn
Paul Grimm	Terrence Moore	G. Bernard Williams
Charles Drum Grinnell	James Moseley	Clayton Porter Wood
Thomas J. Harkey	Maurice George Mueller	Burr Lynch Young
Melvin Harris	Robert Arthur Muir	
Vernon A. Heidinger	Anthony Mulroy	

His greatest challenge was to manage change. In the post–World War II era, the district was in the middle of a building boom: Douglass Elementary School, Webster Groves Memorial Field ("Forty Acres"), and a swimming pool at South Elm and Glendale Road. In January 1947, a delay in construction of the major gymnasium and high school cafeteria brought changes in schedules, location, and duration of gym classes and lunch periods for the high school's 1,700 students.

Turkey Day, 1948, was held in the newly dedicated War Memorial Field.

Labor difficulties and a shortage of steel slowed progress on the construction of Roberts Gym.

Thousands attended the open house of the Charles A. Roberts Gymnasium on December 8, 1947. They marveled at the "last word" in the beauty and structure of the facility containing a balcony and bleacher seats for 1,500, with roll-back bleachers accommodating 500 more. They beamed at the 11,000 square-foot cafeteria beneath the gymnasium that would serve 900 to 1,000 students in two thirty-minute lunch shifts. Heartbreak came when the nervous Statesmen team lost their first home basketball game to the Maplewood Blue Devils on December 18, 1947.

Then came the new electric Baldwin organ at the December 1947 Christmas Candlelight Vesper Services. The organ had been purchased with $4,100 donated by community residents, alumni, and service organizations. Three instead of two services were planned for the capacity crowds forming a waiting line in the new Roberts Gym.

Coach Ray Moss emerged as Charlie Roberts' worthy successor. The charismatic leader was appointed head basketball coach in 1940, but he remained at heart a football man. He had grown up in Boone County, Missouri, where he starred in baseball and track, but he did not play football until he went to Missouri's Moberly Junior College and later the University of Missouri on an athletic scholarship. Afterwards, he coached football at Monett High School in southwest Missouri for one year before coming to Webster Groves.

During his first nine years as Webster Groves High School Statesmen football coach, Ray Moss accumulated a season record of 48 wins, 28 losses, and 6 ties. Standout years included 1941, when he won 6 games and lost 2. He repeated this record in 1944, and in 1945, he earned his best record of 8 wins and 1 tie. His 1940s football legends included Don Keller, Dick Gilman, Shelley Paschens, Carl Deutch, Jim Sprick, Charles Stephens, and Bill Gersting.

Before his retirement in 1975, he had coached basketball, baseball, and varsity football for twenty-five years and served as physical education chairperson and athletic director. Moss Field, formerly Memorial Field, was dedicated to Mr. Ray Moss on October 2, 1976.

By 1948, Webster Groves High School began focusing on the practical arts, beginning with expansion of the industrial arts program. Floor space was doubled, facilities remodeled, new machinery added, new faculty hired, and new courses were offered for boys and girls in grades 8 through 12. Also, the revised curriculum included electronics and welding as well as woodworking, mechanical drawing, and general shop. "Homemaking education" paralleled the program in industrial arts and was "fully launched" in the 1949 school year.

Drivers' education was also added in the fall of 1948. Jim Endicott of Webster Groves' Endicott Chevrolet delivered the new four-door, dual-control sedan. High school teacher August ("Gus")

Prior to the Belleville game, Coach Moss and his starting lineup go over some plays.

Members of the 1953 home economics class engage in a dressmaking project.

Curtis Meeks assists a student with the drivotrainer.

Lamar taught the new drivers' education course to eleventh graders. By 1949, 107 students and two teachers had learned to drive in Mr. Lamar's class, which was opened to all senior high students the following year.

Also in 1949, the Webster Groves School Board began making a color 16-mm film chronicling life in the Webster Groves High School and tentatively titled "The Ten Imperative Needs of Youth," and their list set the tone for the secondary curriculum in the approaching decade.

The "needs" included "saleable skills, health, citizenship, family life, consumer education, science, aesthetics, leisure, ethical values, rationality, and articulation." Curriculum and instruction would show education "at work"—whether in English, mathematics, social studies, art, or business courses in the 1950s movement toward standards, accountability, and performance-based assessment.

Mr. Latta encouraged innovation and believed that team teaching, audio-visual aids, flexible independent study, and "unlimited library use" were the wave of the future in education for eager and restless students. He had found an ally in Superintendent Steger, who believed that child and adolescent development was the key to learning.

In an April 17, 1950 *Webster News-Times* newspaper interview, Dr. Steger stated, "We are trying more and more to center on the problems of adolescent youth." He targeted five areas for application: natural and biological sciences, mathematics, social studies, practical arts (industrial arts and home economics), and the fine arts (art, music, and drama). He added, "We are not just teaching 'cold courses' but general knowledge."

The high school added a work-experience course, called "diversified occupations," in 1950. The program was open to students sixteen years of age who were interested in specialized training and work experience while enrolled in high school. The State of Missouri began the program in 1934, and by 1949, seventy high schools and 2,000 students were enrolled in the program in school districts such as University City, Normandy, Maplewood, Affton, and St. Charles.

An advocate for the practical arts and fine arts as part of the curriculum, Mr. Latta told a *St. Louis Globe-Democrat* interviewer in January 1950: "Years ago there were two main fields of study in our high schools, the classical and the business course. It was folly to send a man into the business world with a narrow preparation. Now it seems that we are meeting the varying needs of the students, and as a result, are building onto them as well as guiding them toward the future."

There was time for fun. The Twelfth-Grade Mothers Club instituted the all-night graduation party in the high school gymnasium in the early 1950s, and by the 1960s, the all-night party would become an elaborate tradition. The idea started with finding a way to curb a night of reckless partying. Students could still have fun but with supervision and decorations along with a fancy supper, swim party, dancing, and a host of imaginative activities.

The basketball team was winning, thanks to Coach Tyke Yates. In the 1952–53 school year, the Statesmen had their best season with a record twenty-seven straight wins, a season record of 28–1, and third place in the State Basketball Tournament, when they lost to Cleveland High School in a game that many considered the Webster Groves Statesmen to be superior to the Cleveland Dutchmen. Yates

The DECA students gather to learn about nursing careers.

graduated from Westminster College in Fulton, Missouri, where he played basketball, and he earned a master's degree from the University of Missouri. Before coming to Webster Groves High School in 1941, he coached at Centralia and Elvins high schools in Missouri. At Webster Groves High School, he served as head basketball and golf coach and was later appointed as dean of students. A March 26, 1953, *Echo* offered this sketch of him:

> He took victory, with it heights of elation for the team, and defeat in his stride. The whole school heard him on several occasions talk in his person-to-person style. In a time when many are in a frequent state of emotional agitation, and letting everyone else become acquainted with their problems, a man of Mr. Yates' nature is indispensable.

When Mr. Yates retired from coaching in 1965 and accepted an administrative post at his alma mater, Westminster College, in 1966, he repaid Webster Groves the compliment: "The community attitude toward sports makes Webster a good place to coach. Parents always have allowed the athletic program to stand on its own merits as a benefit to the students."

Among the "academic" faculty, Mr. George Brucker gained popularity as a mathematics prodigy and scholar in residence. He sponsored the Fencing Club, Bridge Club, Student Council, and *Echo* annual. He served for a while as dean of students before returning to teaching and chairing the Mathematics Department. In October 1963, he received a $1,000 prize as an outstanding secondary school teacher

The Hixson Gym, scene of the annual all-night party, is turned into a magical destination each year by the Senior Parent Club.

(chosen by alumnus Roger Knaus), awarded during Yale University Parents Day ceremonies.

Mr. Brucker had graduated from the University of Illinois in 1940 and was selected by Kappa Delta Pi as the outstanding senior in the College of Education. He began teaching at Troy, Illinois, and later served in the Army Quartermaster Corps and eventually in Japan. After military service, he taught in a veterans' program before returning to the University of Illinois to earn his master's degree in mathematics and again graduating with honors.

He viewed the teaching of mathematics as the teaching of ideas and believed that mathematics instruction should be communicated clearly and precisely. While making mathematics accessible to every student, he instituted an honors course to stimulate the thinking of the more "academically able" student, not only at Webster Groves High School but also at the Mark Twain Institute, where he taught summer courses. Mr. Brucker was a tough, demanding but also highly influential teacher whose students often chose math-oriented careers.

He was an early proponent of the "New Math" in 1966, not as a replacement for traditional mathematics but as a natural "evolution" of math in a changing world rather than as a fixed entity. "Who knows what problems the architect, physicist or engineer will face in the next 10 years?" he asked. "I'm sure that 20 years ago few people could predict our accomplishments in space. And once we begin exploring space we cannot be sure that, for instance, the principles of Euclidean geometry will apply away from earth."

For the present, the elementary school population in Webster Groves had been climbing since the war, prompting building expansion and new schools altogether—Douglass, Washington Park, Goodall, Clark, and more recently Edgar Road. New homes in Webster Groves, Rock Hill, Shrewsbury, Warson Woods, and Glendale brought more students, and more students brought budget, staff, and space constraints for a district long contending with bridging the gap between enrollment and revenue.

This rising tide of students against a scarcity of resources had implications for Webster Groves High School. The population growth for grades 7 through 12 was estimated at 1,040 students by the 1959–60 school year, with another 550 students expected by 1964–65. This increase would require sixty additional teachers and, by 1960, two junior high schools.

What began as a financial and population need mushroomed into a divisive community debate. The Webster Groves School Board set November 17, 1953, as the date for a major bond issue. If passed, $1,665,000 of $2,600,000 would be used to build a new junior high school at 630 South Elm to prevent overcrowding in the high school's lower division. Passage of the bond issue would allow completion of the new Webster Groves Junior High School in September 1955.

Coach Yates and the team celebrate their 55–49 victory over the Billikens in the regional finals. The victory earned the Statesmen a trip to Columbia for the Final Four.

On May 1, 1954, architectural drawings were advertised. On May 2, contracts were let. But on May 17, 1954, the U.S. Supreme Court issued a ruling that would change the Webster Groves School District and the nation's public schools forever. The decision in *Brown v. the Board of Education of Topeka, Kansas* declared the country's racially segregated schools unconstitutional. In Webster Groves, the 1954–55 school year proceeded as usual, and the new junior high school was named for Mr. James T. Hixson, former high school principal and current substitute teacher.

Impending school integration compounded the dilemma of overcrowding at the high school. Current enrollment was 2,200 students. If all went smoothly, the new junior high school would be ready by September 1955. If work were delayed, high school facilities would be severely strained. Even so, Douglass High School's local students needed to enroll—109 in grades 7 through 9, and 87 in grades 10 through 12.

Amid the confusion and ruminations, Coach Ray Moss's "Dream Team," the 1954 undefeated varsity football Statesmen, rose to Missouri Champions and won their twenty-fifth Turkey Day victory over the Kirkwood Pioneers.

Again, Mr. Latta stayed the course. His quiet but effective leadership was recognized outside Webster Groves, when in November 1954, he was elected president of the Missouri Secondary Schools Association and also commissioner of the North Central Association. He had previously served as president of the St. Louis County District Teachers Association in 1951–52.

Hixson Junior High School opened on the first of September 1955, but Douglass High School's merger with Webster Groves High School was delayed until the fall of 1956. The School Board appealed to

Mr. Brucker and friends arrive to chaperone the Paper Doll Prom.

The students of the Webster Groves School District say thank you to the voters for their passage of a tax levy.

residents for passage of a "final" $2,850,000 bond issue, this time for additional facilities at designated elementary schools, for a new Warson Woods Elementary School, and for a new "North Junior High School" at Brownbert Lane and North Rock Hill Road.

In the summer of 1956, Superintendent Leonard A. Steger died of a heart attack at age fifty-two, and Mr. Latta planned for the arrival of Douglass High School students in grades 10 through 12. The community split over whether to build one or two junior high schools, given the reluctance of some residents to send their children to the north section.

Time was running short, and the 1958–59 school year was the last year that the high school could accommodate junior and senior high school students without modified or half-day schedules. But the new bond issue was in jeopardy, and in this era of school integration, no one dared mention publicly the topic of race.

Those taking a middle course argued geography and accessibility, not race. Yet the bond issue failed in April 1956 and again in February 1957. Dissension continued until voters finally approved by 5 to 1 a special bond issue on May 8 to build *two* junior high schools—one on Brownbert Lane and Rock Hill at a cost of $1,624,500 and the other on Lockwood and Plymouth avenues at a cost of $1,430,500. The April 9, 1958 *St. Louis Post-Dispatch* reported this provision: "Boundaries of the two junior high school areas under the current proposal would approximately bisect the Negro neighborhood in the area in question, so that about half the pupils would attend the new schools." The issue was not about race but geography and accessibility. Proof lay in the boundaries of the "bisected" neighborhood. Three junior high schools opened in the fall of 1960: Hixson, Plymouth, and Steger for students in grades 7 through 9. The district's eighth school superintendent, Dr. Herbert W. Schooling, described junior high school as a "bridge" between elementary and high school, allowing the student earlier orientation into more departmentalized schooling with a variety of teachers. He credited Harvard University President Charles Eliot for introducing the concept of the junior high school in American education.

Mr. Hixson died on September 19, 1960, while Webster Groves High School entered the modern era. Enrollment in the fall of 1961 stood at 1,490 and was projected to grow from 2,000 to 2,300 by 1965. Mr. Latta's dream of innovative teaching at the high school was taking shape in more laboratory instruction, team teaching, and a guidance and counseling program. Staff turnover remained a concern, but more pressing was the need for expansion and modernization of facilities that were last updated in the 1920s.

Renovations required the majority of a March 1963 $3,495,000 district-proposed bond issue. A three-story addition constituted the major change. Other improvements included library expansion, additional science and foreign language laboratories, study centers, a health clinic, a guidance department, and more space for administrative services and teacher work areas.

Additional space was needed for art classes and industrial arts, for outdoor physical education, and

Architects' drawing shows the proposed high school addition   Photo by Chet Hanchett

The Webster Echo

Vol. XLIV, No. 8   Webster Groves High School, Webster Groves, Mo.   March 13, 1963

Voters Approve Expansion Plans

Bond Issue Calls For $3,500,000; Hamsher, Grade Schools To Benefit

The $3,5000,000 bond issue, passed last week by Webster school district voters, will finance a 25-room high school addition north of Roberts Gym and east of the main part of the building. The funds will also be used to remodel the old section of the high school, as well as to finance new construction at five elementary schools.

Dr. H.W. Schooling, superintendent of schools, emphasized the key phrase of the campaign last week when he said the bond issue was necessary to "maintain" the quality of education in the district's public schools.

Mr. Joy Whitener, assistant superintendent and public relations man for the school board, said that the bond issue would provide for the expected increase in enrollment. He said the three big problems of the high school--space, adaptation, and modernization--would be solved by the proposed program.

Chemistry teacher, Mr. Kenneth Fast, said of the bond issue, "I'm sorry it didn't happen sooner." He also wished the program could include more expansion. "Let's face it," he said, "We just don't have enough room around here." Of the present students, only the sophomores will be able to use the new expansion, although the juniors will be able to sidewalk superintend the construction. "The new addition may be ready in the fall of 1964," Mr. Whitener estimated. Classes will then move into the new building and the old section will be remodeled.

Plans for school expansion have been considered since 1960, when a committee of citizens made a study of school facilities. This fall an architectural firm, P. John Hoehner and Associates, made definite floor plan sketches. These plans, Mr. Whitener said, "have been a cooperative enterprise of the citizens, the staff, the architects, and the board."

The teachers made specific suggestions to the architects about classroom layouts and arrangements. In the chemistry department, for example, Mr. Fast and Mr. Boyd worked with the architectural firm to design labs.

Dancers Plan Program

The Modern Dance Club will present its fourth annual spring program, May 17 and 18 in the auditorium. The cast is made up of 40 to 50 girls. Dances for the presentation will interpret the four seasons of the year. Another feature portion will include impressions of St. Louis.

Preparation for the program is already under way. Club members are rehearsing the different acts, and planning choreography, costumes, and dances. Mrs. Suzanne Bushey, the club sponsor and modern dance teacher, will direct the program. Mr. Coon, pianist for the dance classes, will accompany the interpretations on the organ and the marimba.

Mrs. Betty Phillips, a music teacher, composed the music for the St. Louis theme. The interpretations will be of various places of interest in and around the city, such as Gaslight Square, Forest Park, the zoo, the park fountains, the memorial arch, and the express highway.

Committee chairman for the program are Naomi Giger, publicity; Mary Bowen, tickets; and scenery, Alice Boothby.

Bell Telephone Honors Seniors

Susan and Charles Munch, twins, share several honors this year. Ranking first and second, respectively, in the Senior Class, they were both invited to attend Southwestern Bell Telephone Company's annual Science Recognition Day Friday, March 1.

The purpose of Science Recognition Day is to encourage students who do well in math and science to develop their interest in these fields. Each year outstanding science and math students from various St. Louis high schools attend the program. However, because of their outstanding scholastic work, Mr. Latta asked to send both students.

During the day, photographers followed the students and, as Charles said, were always "popping out of places."

YMCA Corrects 1963 Buzz Book

Corrections for the 1963 Buzz Book are as follows:

Tenth grade--Anne Brooks, WO 2-4366; Chris Carney, WO 1-4107; Bern Fechter; Gayle Lemcke, WO 1-8987; Bill Mikkelsen; Michael Phelan, WO 2-1627; Vicki Pring, 1013 N. Rock Hill Road; Jane Ward, WO 2-4536; and Mary Cay Warren, WO 1-7344.

Eleventh grade--Mike Harris, 625 Flanders Drive, TA 1-0955; Donna Landry; Joan Marlow, 121 Jefferson Road; Susan Rehkopf; Hal Schnedler; Suzi Specking; Carolyn and Cathy Vesper, WO 1-2851; Patricia Wolff, 405 Belleview; and Chris Woods, 110 N. Elm, WO 1-1030.

Twelfth grade--Sue Birkett, 456 Foreston Place, WO 2-9314; Butch Enslin, 335 Papin; Becky Fauth, Eden Seminary, WO 2-6400; Pat Harris, 625 Flanders Drive, Ta 1-0955; Donna Kiefer, W 1-5809; Lana Krueger, 467a Alma, WO 1-0439; Marion Scatcherd; and Marian Watson, 1202 Eastbrook.

Band Program Raises $4100

In an effort to reach their $7000 goal for new uniforms, the band presented the first of two pops Friday, March 1. Approximately $4100 was collected through the sale of tickets, contributions from business and service clubs, and individual donations.

Seventeen Are Merit Finalists

Seventeen seniors have qualified as National Merit Scholarship finalists.

They are Betsey Anderson, Ellen Detering, Marg Eggers, Bob Grant, Sandy Granville, Lesly Holyoke, Margaret Melick, Charles Munch, Susan Munch, Don Polley, Jean Rimbach, Shelby Robert, Bob Sindel, George Stalker, Carol Stern, Doug Wagner, and John Withers.

All Webster semifinalists qualified as finalists on the basis of Scholastic Aptitude Test scores and the endorsement of the school administration.

Approximately ten percent of all national finalists will win scholarships ranging from $100 to $1500 annually.

Most of the money for these scholarships will come from the Ford Foundation. The amount allocated for the 1962-63 National Merit Scholars is over $2,000,000. However, additional awards are sponsored by various business organizations and individuals. At present there are more than 150 additional scholarships available.

Athletes Establish Lettermen's Club

Five varsity athletes met March 2 to establish a Lettermen's Club to further varsity athletics and symbols, to encourage good sportsmanship, and to develop school spirit throughout the student body.

The formation committee, Allan Curtis, Tom Lanter, Neal Losse, Rick Smith, and Mike Williams, chose Mr. Howard Latta, Mr. Ray Moss, Mr. Robert Smith, and Mr. Tyke Yates as the advisory panel.

Any major letterman will be eligible for the club. All will be notified of the next meeting.

Seniors Choose Special Maids

Seniors Barb Brown, Anita Collins, Judy Evans, Jeanne Marshall, Ann Tweedie, and Betsy Witler were chosen special ECHO maids by the Senior Class February 6.

They were selected from the 24 maids chosen by the class February 4. February 8 the student body selected the ECHO queen from the special maids.

Like the veiled Prophet Queen, her identity is not revealed until the night of the ECHO coronation, April 27. She will be crowned by yearbook editor Alan Hause in Roberts Gym. Jill Newburg, the retiring queen, will also be present.

Theater To Host Dramatic Meet

The Webster Groves Little Theater will serve as host to seven other schools participating in the St. Louis Dramatic-Speech Meet on Saturday, March 16. Each school will present a scene from a play in the dramatic section of the Meet.

Among the seven visiting schools will be Ritenour; Hazlewood, which will do a scene from Tennessee Williams' "The Property is Condemned"; and Mehlville, with a cutting from THE DIARY OF ANNE FRANK.

St. Charles will present a scene from THE GLASS MENAGERIE, also by Tennessee Williams; Riverview Gardens, a scene from Thornton Wilder's OUR TOWN; St. Louis University, a cutting from a HATFUL OF RAIN; and Maryhurst, a scene from THE MIGHTY HUNTER.

The Webster production will be a scene from THE MIRACLE WORKER by Gibson.

A Cappella Choir To Give Broadway Hit 'Brigadoon' Musical Presentation Climaxes Many Weeks' Work

Photo by Chet Hanchett

BRIGADOON cast members are, l. to r., Nancy Denckhoff, Kathy Kuehn, Janet Wurth, and Sue Kice.

BRIGADOON, a musical by Lerner and Lowe will be presented by the Webster Groves High School A Cappella Choir, March 29 and 30, at 8 P.M.

The story, a popular Broadway hit a few years ago, deals with two American boys, Jeff, played by Tom Alt; and Tom, played by John Dougherty, who, lost in the woods of Scotland, accidentally find themselves in the center of an uncharted village--Brigadoon.

During the bustle of market day, they quickly become acquainted with the residents and their problems. They meet petulant Harry Beaton, played by Scott Davis; Jean and Fiona McClarren, portrayed by Janet Wurth and Sue Kice; infatuated Charles Dalrymple, played by Tom Pope; and Meg, played by Kathy Kuehn.

During their visit, both boys fall in love, become involved in a rollicking wedding celebration, take part in a man-hunt, and gain a better understanding and faith in human nature.

Some of the better known songs in the musical include "It's Almost Like Being in Love", "Come to Me, Bend to Me", and "What A Day This Has Been".

Since the beginning of the semester, the choir, directed by Miss Esther Replogle, has been working hard on the show. After a few weeks delay due to indecision concerning the choice of the operetta, the arrival of the music, and the selection of the cast, rehearsals began in earnest.

Admission to the production will again be on a reserved-seat basis. Tickets, which can be purchased from any A Cappella Choir member.

The *Echo* heralds the expansion of the high school.

A CBS cameraman prepares to shoot a student interview.

for parking areas, which required purchase of residential property along Selma Avenue.

The demands the future will make on today's children are difficult to predict, but it is evident that the advances of science and technology will require new skills and the problem of establishing peaceful relationships with other peoples will require greater knowledge and understanding than the past.

For Dr. Schooling, the expansion was an investment in quality education. Before coming to Webster Groves in 1957, he had served as superintendent in North Kansas City and as director of the University of Chicago Laboratory School. He held an undergraduate degree from Southeast Missouri State College and a master's degree from the University of Missouri.

Regarded as an expert on school administration and later dean of the School of Education at the University of Missouri, Dr. Schooling insisted that school quality depends on local initiative. He cited three conditions making Webster Groves a "superior" school district: 1) the support of the School Board, 2) the respect of the professional staff, and 3) the high community expectations for its schools.

In the 1960s, Webster Groves High School became "a school of the future" with quality teaching, research-based curriculum and technology, and student-centered instruction. The Chemistry Department led the way, and the English, Foreign Language, and Science Departments soon followed.

The Chemistry Department's adoption of a new CHEM Program began an inquiry-based approach to teaching science. A byproduct of the National Science Foundation in the post-Sputnik era, the program used a textbook and manual incorporating the expertise and practices of leading chemists. The idea was to simulate how chemists work in a laboratory rather than memorizing formulas and elements.

The teacher acts as a "consultant," and tests are often open-book, as students make their own discoveries. Audiovisuals such as models and films are used to explain or amplify concepts, but students are encouraged to discuss and to think in instruction stressing methodology as well as content.

The quality showed. In 1964, Webster Groves High School ranked second in the state for the most graduates earning doctoral degrees, according to the National Research Council of the National Academy of Sciences. From 1959 to 1962, the number of Webster alumni earning doctorates totaled twenty-five, most of them in the fields of chemistry, economics, and education. The study suggested that while the size of the school is a factor in the number of students receiving advanced degrees, so is the quality of high school experiences in preparing students and shaping career decisions.

Nothing excited the community more in the fall of 1965 than the filming of the planned hour-long CBS (Columbia Broadcasting System) television documentary. According to sociologist and producer Dr. Arthur Barron, the purpose of the documentary was to show what it was like to be a sixteen-year-old student in Webster Groves, particularly during the junior year in high school. Before the documentary aired on February 8, 1966, the television crew had twenty-two hours of footage from their twelve-week "study" of 688 sixteen-year-olds and had spent a total of $130,000.

The late 1960s showed a broadening of student interests.

Time and cost were incidental compared to the controversy the film ultimately sparked in Webster Groves. Dr. Barron led local residents to believe that his findings—based on a questionnaire, interviews, and observations—indicated "average teenagers" in a "typical" midwestern middle-class suburb. The study addressed issues such as academic pressure, cheating, dating, social life, parental control, racial relations, and future goals.

As if an omen, the February 8 showing was postponed after being preempted by a news special on the Vietnam War. District residents resigned themselves to the rescheduling of the documentary, which eventually aired on Friday, February 25.

There was stony silence, then disbelief, followed by outrage and letters to CBS and local newspapers. Not since the mid-1950s junior-high dispute had the community been so divided and shaken. Reactions ranged from irate, accusatory, reflective, and soul-searching, to general, if silent, agreement.

Narrated by Charles Kuralt, the documentary depicted Webster Groves sixteen-year-olds as sheltered, parent-driven teenagers whose primary goals were a "good job, money, and success." Many residents considered the portrayal preconceived, biased, and mean-spirited, particularly in its labeling of Webster Groves High School students as either "socies," "normies," "weirdos," "intellectuals," or "fringe"—with the "socies" ruling the school.

Mr. Latta took a diplomatic stance: "I suppose it depends from what viewpoint you look at it, but I would say it was quite revealing and ought to be helpful to a lot of people." For years he had fretted over students "caught up" in the pursuit of success through a singular social and academic focus instead of a well-rounded education geared toward learning how to live.

CBS offered a followup airing on April 8 called "An Evening with the St. James' and MacGreevys," but by then the voices of students and residents rang hollow, and years later, few viewers recalled anything except the original broadcast.

Except for the annual Turkey Day Game and Christmas Vespers service, there was no return to normalcy at Webster Groves High School. For draft-conscious seniors approaching graduation, a war escalated in Vietnam. For a school struggling to include African American students in its upper-level classes and extracurricular clubs, a national civil rights campaign was gaining momentum. Outspoken staffers on the student *Echo* newspaper continued its time-honored tradition of questioning the status quo.

The tone grew more serious and selfless in a school embracing community service, travel exchange programs, participation in the KXOK College Bowl, and a new school paperback bookstore. The "intellectuals," "weirdos," and "fringes" were gaining ground.

The paperback bookstore opened in the fall of 1966, before school and during lunch, and was staffed by English teacher Mr. Bill Mathes and student volunteers. The store sold 1,500 books the first three weeks. Students bought English versions of Flaubert's *Madame Bovary* and Vergil's *Aeneid*. They not only bought Edith Hamilton's *The Roman Way* and *The Greek Way* but also *One Hundred and One Elephant Jokes* and *Mad*. They bought vocabulary and grammar simplified texts as well as *The Hobbit* and *The Lord of the Rings* trilogy.

The new Senior Lounge opened on October 13, 1966, with a surprise unveiling of a portrait of Mr. Latta. His portrait previously hung in the hallway, but Mr. Latta, a modest man, removed and hid it behind a file cabinet in his office. Seniors paid for carpeting in the lounge with Eagle Stamp book collections. Student class officers supervised the lounge but gave most of the credit to their sponsor, speech teacher Mrs. Dorothy Weirich.

Mr. Latta retired in 1968, following thirty-seven years of district service and twenty-five years as Webster Groves High School principal. The Student Council created a scholarship in his honor, and faculty and students agreed that he had lived up to Superintendent Willard Goslin's prediction in a letter in 1943: "I think you have a great future ahead of you. Under your leadership this ought to be one of the outstanding secondary schools in the country for a period of the next good many years."

Five hundred and eighty seniors graduated in the Class of 1968—Mr. Latta's final year. The class theme was "The Generation Gap."

Chapter 6

> *"Hamsher High School is a school where students are striving along with staff to help give direction to their own education. This makes the challenge of the principalship of this school exciting."*
> —Jerry Knight

GERALD E. KUSLER

In the fall of 1968, Gerald E. Kusler, the new high school principal, faced 2,012 students in grades 10 through 12. He found a high school ranking among the top in standardized test scores, National Merit Scholars, college-bound graduates, athletic and arts competitions, and faculty with advanced degrees. He also discovered racial stratification, waning student involvement, faculty entrenchment, and lagging support for the practical arts.

Before coming to Webster Groves, Mr. Kusler had served two years as principal in East Lansing, Michigan. He earned bachelor and master's degrees in English from the State University of Iowa. He taught English in Aurora, Illinois, and served as department chair and administrative assistant in Hinsdale, Illinois. He completed post-graduate work as a John Hay Fellow at Northwestern University and in English at the University of Illinois and Michigan State University.

As Webster Groves High School's fourth principal, he listened and implemented. African American students were elected to student government and cheerleading squads. Faculty room changes discouraged territoriality and complacency. Faculty participation in student enrollment led to wiser course selections. The North Central Association Visiting Committee made additional recommendations.

Six major student-faculty initiatives grew out of the 1968–69 school year: organization of a Human Relations Board as a branch of student government, formation of the Students for Black Awareness and Action Club, development of a senior exchange program with Vashon High School, presentation of the first predominantly African American play at Webster Groves High School, the organization of the American Field Service (AFS) Club, and the debut of the high school's spring Fine Arts Festival.

Created for "student betterment," the Human Relations Board dealt with student problems, ranging from race relations to student dress. Students for Black Awareness and Action (SBAA), an interracial group open to all students, sponsored speakers and raised money for senior scholarships. The group also raised money for relief efforts in Biafra.

Mr. Kusler spent the day discussing school issues with interested seniors in the lounge.

Increased enrollment made negotiating the hallways a challenge.

facing page: On their way to a state title, the 1979 football Statesmen defeated Kirkwood on Turkey Day and once again brought the bell home.

The Biafra drive got underway as the members of SBAA sort and box food and clothing items.

The AFS Coca-Cola party allowed the students of WGHS to meet the foreign exchange students and learn about their countries.

Lorraine Hansberry's *A Raisin in the Sun* was performed on March 14, 15, and 17, 1969, in the Little Theater. The play was produced by drama teacher Mrs. Ernestine Smizer and directed by English Department chair and teacher Mrs. Mildred Fredericksen. The performance marked the Webster Groves High School's first play by a predominantly African American student cast and the first work by an African American playwright. Principal cast members included Ella Redmond as Lena Younger, Charles Thomas as Walter Lee Younger, Cheryl Black as Beneatha Younger, Brenda Tripp as Ruth Younger, Kevin Brackens as Travis Younger, and Gary Miller as Karl Lindner.

The senior class sponsored a cultural exchange program with Vashon High School in St. Louis City. Twenty-five to thirty-five students from Webster Groves High School and forty-five students from Vashon participated in all-day visits to discuss mutual problems and solutions, advantages and disadvantages of majority and minority status, and ways the two groups could help each other. Faculty sponsor Dorothy Weirich stated that Vashon was selected because its African American student ratio was the "reverse" of Webster Groves High School.

The American Field Service Club (AFS) organized in March 1969 to promote awareness of the program, to welcome foreign exchange students, and to raise money and help find homes for participants. An annual spaghetti supper became their primary fundraiser.

The Fine Arts Festival opened in mid-May 1969 "to expose students to all forms and levels of the fine arts: visual art, drama, literature, and music." The Drama Department presented two plays in the Little Theater. Artwork was displayed in the library and throughout the school, and student and faculty artists offered demonstrations. Vocal music and modern dance programs were performed in the auditorium. Speech classes presented readings while guest speakers offered sessions on various topics. Free movies or classic films were shown, and after-school programs showcased community and student musicians, dancers, and artists.

Forty-two visiting members representing the North Central Association (NCA) arrived in December 1968 to review the high school's self-assessment of its resident community, philosophy, school program, physical plant, and facilities. The NCA process occurred every seven years and involved a three-year preparation and response program for the school. The first year was devoted to home committee study, the second year to the visiting committees, and the third year to home committee review and implementation of recommendations.

Areas for improvement were a wider program for non-college-bound students, renovation of the Industrial Arts Department, and more student-centered and innovative classroom instruction.

The first all-black cast presented the Broadway hit *A Raisin in the Sun.*

The advanced art students "plastered" classmates for display at the Art Festival.

May 4-5

A creative showcase, the Arts Festival put WGHS musicians, vocalists, actors, mimes, and visual artists front stage, as they displayed their talents in the courtyard, theater, and Selma Field.

In a year filled with change, 1968–69 would hold a final surprise: the resignation of Mr. Kusler. He resumed his position as principal of East Lansing High School, but he left Webster Groves with a tribute and exhortation. In an open letter to students and faculty in the *Echo*, he wrote:

> *Loyalty, spirit, tradition are permeating qualities here. Respect for one another is a visible characteristic of this student body. The ability to accept and discharge greater responsibility is also clear.*
>
> *Perhaps the most exciting and challenging "plus" in this school right now is the increased awareness of the need for change. One sees students agitating for the greater role for racial and social "outsiders." One sees students unwilling to accept the old model for student government. One sees student groups looking for ways to "humanize" the school experience and for ways to contribute student thought to curriculum planning.*
>
> *One sees teachers adopting new materials and trying new methods. One sees a faculty committed to a search for ways to vary instruction and to developing meaningful programs for all students.*
>
> *I believe that, with the outstanding human resources in the faculty and student body and the great interest and support of the community, you will continue to make Webster a school to be proud of. I shall always be proud to have been here.*

JERRY KNIGHT

Orderly change defined the leadership of Jerry R. Knight, Webster Groves High School's fifth principal. In the fall of 1969, the 6'5" former college basketball player faced the shifting tides of educational experimentation, the peak and decline of student enrollment, federal antidiscrimination mandates, state testing and monitoring, funding shortfalls, and faculty cutbacks.

He was no stranger to the district. For three years Mr. Knight served as principal of Steger Junior High School. Before then, he spent ten years in the Ritenour School District in northwest St. Louis County, where he worked as a math teacher, counselor, and assistant principal of Hoech Junior High School. He held a bachelor's degree in mathematics from Missouri Valley College in Marshall, Missouri, and a master's degree in education from Washington University in St. Louis.

Despite his firm grip on student discipline, Mr. Knight gained respect for his willingness to consider new ideas. During his leadership in the 1970s, the high school moved to a more decentralized curriculum, open-campus lunch system, relaxed dress code, self-policing student smoking area, senior class meetings, and Principal's Advisory Council.

The Science Department led curriculum innovations. Its discovery-learning method inspired high-interest courses in other departments. The English Department replaced most of its yearlong courses with semester and nine-week quarter courses such as Fantasy and Science Fiction, Shakespeare, Mythology and Folklore, Dissent, Black Literature, and From Franklin to Faulkner, using a thematic or cultural approach to the study of language and literature.

A senior humanities course used an inquiry approach to investigate Western and non-Western history, cultures, religions, and literatures. Faculty teams from social studies, English, drama, art, and music taught the two-hour course and used small and larger-group instruction, guest speakers, and field trips to allow students to experience other cultures. Near the end of the school year, student teams created their own societies.

The Art Department adopted a "studio approach," allowing students to work at their own levels. The Industrial Arts Department broadened curriculum in power technology, electricity-electronics, metals and drafting, and added a course in marine power. The Business Department offered office practice and office work-experience for job-related training. The Physical Education Department experimented with team and individual sports instruction while continuing its modern dance program.

The Social Studies Department used a moral values curriculum to study public issues through historical analysis. The Math Department adopted a computer-assisted mathematics program and offered a practical mathematics course for non-college-bound students. The Music Department continued its fall musical, winter and spring concerts, and regional and state competitions. Spanish emerged as the most popular language offering in the Foreign Language Department.

In the practical arts, child development, consumer education, and interior design became part of the home economics curriculum. Driver Education offered simulated driving and "on the road" experience for five hundred students.

Student Council remained the "driving force" of the school, moving from a "social organization" to a school leadership and service organization. It sponsored the Free Study Program, an honor-system study hall, and raised money through school-wide magazine sales. It assumed responsibility for the bonfire for Turkey Day. It collected food for Christmas baskets for the underprivileged and sponsored a talent show to raise money for the Howard A. Latta Scholarship Fund.

The Senior Class Cabinet continued its cultural exchange with a city high school, with Soldan instead of Vashon. The James T. Hixson Club, a chartered club of the Future Teachers of America, explored the field of teaching through guest speakers, films, and teacher assistantships.

The St. Louis Leadership Project allowed student representatives from Webster Groves High School to meet monthly with students from area schools to collaborate on communication techniques and problem-solving skills. The Close-Up Program allowed students and teacher chaperones to visit government officials in Washington, D.C., where they learned first-hand about the operations of the federal government.

In the fall of 1971, Webster Groves High School announced nineteen National Merit Semifinalists, more than any other high school in Missouri. The new Community Campus program, "WCC," offered an alternative to classroom instruction. Students earned credit through work related to a future job, college preparation, community service, or student interest. Enrollees chose institutions or agencies such as hospitals, radio and television stations, the Saint Louis Zoo, the Missouri Botanical Garden, area college laboratories, animal shelters, and local elementary schools.

Jerry Knight prepared to meet the NCA visiting committee, who spent several days evaluating the high school's program and facilities.

Jim Martin and Scott Miller mastered the art of baking in their foods class.

For the fourth year in a row, Mr. Brucker's first-hour class took first place in the annual can food drive, collecting 3,700 cans of the 11,117 donated to the needy.

Mrs. Wojak and Mr. Shles visited a community campus student whose internship was located at the Missouri Botanical Garden.

A student performance of Lorraine Hansberry's *A Raisin in the Sun* returned to the Little Theatre stage in April 1972, again with a predominately African American student cast, but this time with a student director, Brenda Tripp. A new "Sixteen in Webster Groves" documentary surfaced in 1974, eight years after the original by CBS, and this time locally produced by KMOX-TV.

The new high school drama teacher, Ron Kenney, like Eugene Wood forty years before, brought as many students to the stage as possible while evoking philosophical questions of actors and audiences. An avid reader, Mr. Kenney arrived at the high school in 1972, already a scholar of Teilhord de Chordin, the twentieth century theologian and philosopher, and a faithful subscriber of *The Village Voice*. He inspired many of his students to pursue professional acting careers while staging such *avant-garde* plays as Harold Pinter's *The Birthday Party*, Langford Wilson's *The Rimers of Eldritch*, and Gore Vidal's *A Visit to a Small Planet*.

The Webster Groves Hockey Club formed in December 1972 and played Kirkwood, Ladue, Lindbergh, DuBourg, Southwest, Lafayette, and Whitfield. Students for Black Awareness and Action joined the Student Service Council in collecting food and toys for the needy before the winter holidays and held a Malcolm X assembly in the spring of 1973. Girls joined the Chess Club. Student artists won Scholastic Art Awards under the guidance of art teacher and nationally ranked artist Marilynne Bradley. The Webster Groves faculty presented a talent show and raised six hundred dollars for the scholarship honoring their special guest: Mr. Howard A. Latta.

The school board grappled with revenue loss, teacher layoffs, and salary freezes, despite bond issue funding for renovation projects that would give faculty and students "more room and better facilities." Girls' field hockey was dropped, and athletic coaches were hard-pressed to cover girls' volleyball and basketball.

In 1974, the choir moved to the Senior Lounge area, and a new lounge was built off the courtyard. A preschool nursery was built where the choir rooms once stood, and a new staircase connected the library to the humanities classrooms on the second floor. Office and storage space was added to the girls' south gym, along with new lockers.

Following months of planning, the first high school Model United Nations convened in March 1974. Delegates used the Webster Groves Presbyterian Fellowship Hall for choosing topics, organizing power blocs, and making posters for meetings. Issues included population control, international terrorism, the oil crisis, cooperative harvesting of world resources, and peacekeeping funding. At home, school vandalism and student drinking loomed as troubling issues.

After girls were permitted to wear pants to school in the 1970s, the fastest growing trend was jeans: Dickies for the girls and Levis for the boys, and the place to buy them was Rudolph's Dry Goods Store. Located in Old Webster on South Gore, the antiquated denim emporium was operated by Dave Rudolph, a Webster Groves High School alumnus, and his wife Rose.

Every customer was a cherished buyer, for whom Mr. Rudolph personally selected the merchandise. Neophytes and veterans alike trailed behind him through mazes of rustic aisles to tables towering with chambray shirts and jeans as stiff as sandpaper. They reminded each customer that "our motto is whatever people can't find elsewhere, they can always find it at Rudolph's."

A Visit to a Small Planet, presented in the fall of 1977, featured the talent of Greg Johnston, John Starmer, and Pearce Wilson.

While the nation coped with inflation and recession, the Webster Groves School District reeled under rising costs and falling enrollment—an 18 percent decline between 1969 and 1974. Fifty-five percent of Webster Groves residents had no children in school, which left a scarcity of homes for new families with children. Superintendent George W. Brown estimated that the $175 per pupil expenditure in 1974 would reach $429 by 1980. Increased state and federal aid seemed the only hope. Staff reduction and consolidation of some elementary schools were the immediate solutions.

The Class of 1974, in the Watergate era, was more socially fragmented and politically disillusioned than earlier graduates. Race relations, however, were "cool," even though black and white students clustered separately in the cafeteria and at the senior and junior entrances. There were also Black Studies courses, a vibrant Student for Black Awareness and Action Club open to black and white students, and more African American teachers since 1968.

On May 11, 1974, Ivory Crockett, Class of 1968, ran the 100-yard dash in 9.0 seconds, breaking the eleven-year-old world record of 9.1 set by Bob Hayes. Crockett's best record at Webster Groves High School was 9.5, and the friendly, hardworking student-athlete had earned a scholarship to Southern Illinois University in Carbondale.

Social studies teacher Ms. Wilda Swift was literally making history. After receiving a $14,060 grant from the National Endowment for the Humanities for the 1975–76 school year, she offered a local history course using legal documents, public records, church records, and library books for student research. The first class chose Webster Groves history from 1900 to 1915 and conducted personal interviews with residents. Swift's classes published four books, titled *In Retrospect*, which remain classics of the Webster Groves' early community and school district.

The 1970s were a casual time, with jeans as the look of choice.

U.S. President Jimmy Carter, in 1977, proposed a minimum wage increase from $2.30 to $2.50 an hour. Paul Farrar, of Webster Groves High School, was considered "the best basketball player in St. Louis," with an average of 26 points and a game-high of 46 points. "Band-Aids," a new high school parent support group, organized to raise money for band uniforms, supplementary equipment, and band trips. A group of faculty and students reactivated the National Honor Society.

High school sports enjoyed a revival. The girls' running team, in 1977, remained undefeated. Martin Eason, in 1978, won the state wrestling championship. In 1979, the Webster Groves Statesmen won

Records fell as Ivory Crockett, Class of 1968, took to the track.

the Class 4A football state championship, beating Jefferson City 7–6. Their season record was 12–1, and victory was sweeter because this was the first year the team was eligible to play for the title. For eleven years of the state championships, the Statesmen previously had opted to play the Turkey Day Game against Kirkwood rather than compete for the state title. Jack Jones was the winning football coach; Andre Nelson was the winning quarterback. Standouts were Joel Blunk, Kenny Buford, Tracey Mack, Terry Jones, "Brick" Johnstone, and Larry Stout. John Keane recovered a key fumble, and Mark Loving scored the winning touchdown.

Ms. Pat Voss, director of activities and assistant principal, became the wind beneath the sails of student organizations. The former social studies teacher possessed strong organizational skills and boundless enthusiasm in guiding student groups through Turkey Day festivities, including the bonfire, pep rally, senior line dance, and decorations. Voss also helped students with planning the Spring Arts Festival.

The district's financial woes continued, along with shrinking enrollment, faculty attrition, and federal enforcement of guidelines for racial balance that required junior high reorganization. From 1969 to 1978, the district's student population dropped from 8,500 to 4,591, while minority enrollment rose by 1 percent. Grades 7 and 8 remained at Hixson and temporarily at Steger. Grade 9 moved to Plymouth Junior High School, and to the high school in 1978.

Webster Groves High School tightened standards and recommitted itself to a wide range of students. Teachers updated curricula. A gifted program and honors classes were added. Ninety-minute semester and final examinations were implemented in 1978, and math proficiency tests in 1979. The School Board increased graduation requirements from twenty credits to twenty-two.

Distributive Education Clubs of America (DECA), a student marketing and business management organization, held its first district-wide conference. The high school's administrative staff reorganized into unit offices with assistant principals, counselors, and secretaries available to address individual student needs. The School Board revised its guidelines and policies for staff and students, and in the fall of 1982, the district reported its lowest decline in twelve years—from 3,779 to 3,658.

The most far-reaching change of the decade came with the 1983 St. Louis City-County school desegregation plan. The program stemmed from a lawsuit, *Liddell v. the Board of Education (of St. Louis)*, dating back to 1972, when Mrs. Minnie Liddell, a black St. Louis City parent and leader of the Concerned Parents of North St. Louis, requested that her son remain in his neighborhood school instead of being bused to another school that was less well equipped.

While Liddell reached a preliminary settlement with the St. Louis School Board in 1975, she was joined in her suit by the U.S. Department of Justice and the national NAACP (National Association for the Advancement of Colored People), which asserted that St. Louis's city schools were racially segregated as a result of law and practice. The Eighth Circuit Court of Appeals heard the case, and the Missouri State Board of Education and Missouri commissioner of education were included as defendants.

Marching in the VP Fair involved hard work, with the reward of some time to chill.

Long straight hair with a headband was the status symbol of the 1970s.

As the final seconds ticked away, the cheerleaders anxiously awaited Webster's first state football title.

Liddell supporters maintained that from 1954 to 1980 the student population in St. Louis Public Schools shifted from predominantly white to predominantly black, producing a pattern of "white flight" to the suburbs. These segregation trends, they insisted, made it impossible for St. Louis City students to receive an education equal to their St. Louis County counterparts.

The State of Missouri, Liddell supporters claimed, contributed to school segregation through laws dating back to 1847, when the state prohibited the education of Missouri black residents. In 1865, the state allowed separate schools for African American children, an arrangement upheld by the 1896 U.S. Supreme Court decision in *Plessy v. Ferguson*, but Missouri did not officially remove the separate schools statute from its constitution until 1976, twenty-two years after the U.S. Supreme Court overturned the practice in *Brown v. the Board of Education of Topeka*.

The Webster Groves School District was named as one of twenty-three suburban districts contributing to area-wide segregation. The list included Affton, Bayless, Brentwood, Ferguson-Florissant, Hancock Place, Hazelwood, Jennings, Ladue, Lindbergh, Maplewood–Richmond Heights, Mehlville, Normandy, Parkway, Riverview Gardens, Rockwood, Valley Park, and Wellston. Five districts—Clayton, Kirkwood, Pattonville, Ritenour, and University City—agreed to a settlement in 1981. The remaining eighteen, including Webster Groves, fought the suit. Their greatest concern was a court-ordered merger of city and county school districts.

Judge William L. Hungate of the United States District Court for the Eastern District of Missouri began hearing the case in 1981, and a plan was finally put in place in the spring of 1983. The Voluntary Interdistrict Transfer Program would allow African American students from St. Louis City to enroll in St. Louis County schools until the suburban districts reached a maximum enrollment of 25 percent minority students. Caucasian students from the county could enroll in city schools at the same percentage. The State of Missouri would pay tuition and transportation costs for a maximum of 15,000 students. The "unique and comprehensive settlement agreement" would be fully implemented by 1984, becoming the largest voluntary interdistrict transfer program in the nation.

The Webster Groves School District enrolled 170 students from St. Louis City in the fall of 1983, and 40 more the following school year, for a total of over 210 students. The district met its legal obligation of 25 percent minority students by the 1984–85 school year, largely due to its resident minority student population. The state no longer funded county magnet programs, such as the video production student lab at Webster Groves High School, and county transfer students to city schools eventually paid for their own tuition and transportation.

Another North Central Association Visiting Committee, in 1983, had come and gone, and Jerry Knight marked changes in the high school's demographics and instruction.

> *Academically, socially, emotionally and economically, our students come from diverse backgrounds. Minorities make up approximately 20 percent of our student body, and a similar percentage of our students come from single parent homes. In addition, a sizeable number of young people attend this school while in residence at Edgewood Children's Home or the United Methodist Children's Home. It is our opinion that this diversity allows our student body to learn, to live, and to get along in a real microcosm of society.*

Yearlong classes replaced quarter courses. Teachers focused on the "basics" as well as exploration of interests. "A-Period" or before-school classes such as music, art, foreign language, or pompons allowed students to earn credit that would not fit into their six-hour schedule. Jerry Knight had guided the high school through a succession of changes from the 1970s through the mid-1980s.

The greatest constant of the era was the ever-changing fashion scene.

Bill Manganaro, co-editor of the *Webster Echo* in 1975, spent a day job-shadowing his principal and filed this summation:

> Jerry R. Knight, Webster High principal: the mention of this name conjures up multifarious visions of Almighty Zeus, seated atop a lofty peak, ready to hurl his thunderbolts of red fire upon those mortals who would defy his rules. He appears thus, powerful and foreboding, in the minds of countless students.
>
> The fact is that Mr. Knight faced a tidal wave of political and social changes during the 1970s, changes which impacted curriculum design, teaching methodology, faculty-student relationships, student enrollment, faculty employment, and community perceptions. His goal was to keep order and educate youth during turbulent times.
>
> Knight's job is one which must combine sternness with compassion and levity. He must attempt to keep the school functioning smoothly along lines which are acceptable to students, staff, and school board. In his role as an intermediary among these groups, Knight performs his task admirably.

When Jerry Knight retired as principal in 1986, he was appointed assistant superintendent in charge of the district's business office. In 1997, the high school's Knight Auditorium honored his thirty years of district service. He was no Zeus, but from 1969 to 1986, his devotion to Webster Groves High School remained unquestioned.

Part III
FORWARD PROGRESS

Chapter 7

"Through these halls walk some of the finest students in the nation."

—Dan Edwards

DAN EDWARDS

The orange and black banner became Dr. Dan Edwards' gift to Webster Groves High School, a testament to his nudging the school from its mid-1980s slumber to reclaim county and statewide distinction as well as national stature.

The former Kirkwood middle school principal began his tenure by meeting with the high school faculty in the spring of 1986. Together, they drafted three goals for the 1986–87 school year: 1) to enhance the school climate by interacting with students and staff; 2) to increase community involvement through group visits to the campus and the use of parent volunteers as tutors or library assistants; and 3) to improve interpersonal relations, starting with the new homeroom advisement program.

An Illinois native, Edwards completed his undergraduate work at Northern Kentucky University, earned a master's degree in administration from Northeast Missouri (Truman) University, and held a doctorate from Saint Louis University. After teaching middle school in Cool Springs, Missouri, he served as assistant principal in the Fort Zumwalt and Kirkwood school districts.

As Webster Groves High School's sixth principal, he adopted a student-oriented approach stressing learning styles, team teaching, curriculum coordination, and student and staff motivation. He appointed a "Committee of Forty"—a cross-section of students—to encourage school spirit, inform the student body of school activities, and to promote academics.

He implemented the Renaissance Program, an incentives initiative begun in Conway, South Carolina, and geared toward "inspiring students to strive for excellence and to recognize faculty and staff members as true professionals." Webster Groves High School became one of the first schools in the country to adopt the program, and Dr. Edwards used extrinsic rewards and public recognition to increase academic achievement.

Staff barbecues and faculty retreats, theater and concert ticket raffles, and school sweatshirts and gear instilled pride, enthusiasm, and unity. Freshmen orientation picnics, student discount cards for high achievers, and school assemblies for honor students celebrated student success. The Eagle Award was established in recognition of one graduating senior who had been nominated and selected

Dr. Edwards greeted students as they entered the high school at the start of each school day.

facing page: Practice makes perfect as the cast of "West Side Story" rehearsed a song and dance.

Exhausted after a challenge course ordeal, Committee of Forty members looked forward to a hot shower and some snacks.

by the staff on the basis of scholarship, leadership, citizenship, character, and community service.

In-school suspension became the alternative to out-of-school suspension. Implemented in January 1987, the program used social isolation instead of academic penalty. Then-Assistant Principal Pat Voss explained the program to the *Echo* newspaper: "A kid who gets in trouble would rather be out of school anyway. By keeping him in school, we don't give him what he wants." Teachers sent assignments to the in-school supervisor to ensure that suspended students completed class work.

Service clubs rallied a new generation of students. STAR, formed in 1986 by social studies teacher Jim Muth, strove to feed the poor and hungry. Concerned faculty, students, and other volunteers gathered after school to make sandwiches and to donate fresh fruit to St. Louis–area charities and food pantries.

Peer Helpers, coordinated by guidance counselor Pam Nickels in 1987, served as a student counseling outreach group. Volunteers participated in a big brother/big sister program with elementary schools, taught HI-STEP self-esteem classes to third graders, worked with the DARE Program's anti-drug and anti-alcohol campaign, and presented informal lectures on teenage health issues in high school classes.

The Red Cross Blood Drive became the annual service project of the National Honor Society (NHS). Approximately 25 percent of the local Red Cross's donated blood came from high school donors, and

Breakfast with Santa benefits the food basket drive sponsored by the Webster–Rock Hill Ministries.

despite the AIDS scare of the late 1980s, the high school's NHS clung to its goal of collecting 170 pints of blood each year.

The national media called again in March 1987, twenty years after CBS's controversial documentary "Sixteen in Webster Groves." ABC News producers wanted to know what life was like for students in the suburbs, and after interviewing twelve seniors and featuring five of them in a five-minute segment, the consensus seemed clear: "We are proud of our town. We have very good schools. We count on family and friends. We never think about silverware."

Despite a lull in school spirit, the high school announced nine National Merit Semifinalists in the fall of 1987. College credit became the incentive in advanced high school classes. Saint Louis University and the University of Missouri at St. Louis offered credit for courses such as honors American history, honors U.S. studies, calculus, art history, advanced physics, advanced Spanish, English literature, and twentieth-century international affairs. High school faculty taught the courses, and students could opt to pay the tuition fee for college credit.

The fall musical *Fiddler on the Roof* opened in November 1987, with a diverse cast and student crew largely in charge of the set, costumes, makeup, and production. Still, art teacher Marilynne Bradley bemoaned sluggish support for the arts with the demise of the annual spring Arts Festival and the low turnouts for art exhibits, drama productions, and music concerts.

The staff challenged the varsity boys and girls basketball teams to a game in front of the entire student body.

English and speech teacher Kay Wojak, before her death in 1989, revived the high school's vaunted debate tradition. In January 1988, seniors Steve Fingerhut, Kelly Dunsford, and A. B. Kelly earned top honors in the Crackerjack Tourney at Parkway South High School. The Lincoln–Douglass debate

The 1993 and 1994 Sweetheart Queens receive congratulations from their friends.

topic was pro/con: "The protection of society's health interests through broad-based mandatory testing for AIDS is more important than personal privacy."

The high school held its first Sweetheart Dance in February 1988. Math teacher Bernice O'Brien's advisement group proposed the dance as a junior class venture to broaden student participation and to promote student unity. Like the fall Friendship Dance, the Sweetheart Dance culminated with the crowning of a king and a queen.

District voters passed a $3.5 million bond issue in March 1988, to fund computer labs, asbestos removal, plumbing and wiring repairs, and energy conservation. School cafeteria services were contracted out to an independent catering company to increase cost-effectiveness and menu variety.

Technology became the order of things. Macintosh computers arrived for *Echo* newspaper production in the fall of 1988, and every high school student was required to obtain an identification card to check out library books, to register for PSAT/SAT/ACT tests, and to receive student discounts.

The athletics program, though, remained strong and steady. Six baseball players (Jim Georgia, Hunter Beckham, Mike Morhaus, Matt Kennkens, Kenny Mesnier, and Chris Johann) traveled to Sydney, Australia, in December 1987 as representatives of the the Stockham American Legion Baseball Team. In the spring of 1988, the high school baseball team's 8–3 record earned them a chance to play state select teams.

The new Judo Club drew thirty-six members of adults, teens, and children. History teacher and later Assistant Principal George White sponsored the club. A third-degree black belt, White explained that Judo was an "artistic sport," inviting the participation of males and females while teaching self-confidence, disciplinary fitness, and self-defense.

Statesmen teams and star athletes ushered in a new championship era. The varsity football team won the state 4-A championship in 1988. Following a shaky start of 1–3, the Statesmen rode an eight-game winning streak to Jefferson City, where they defeated the Kansas City Center Yellow Jackets 26–0. Dan Fugate was the winning quarterback. Chuck Washington scored the first touchdown, Steve Watson made the final touchdown, and Matt Arrandale broke his thirty-nine-yard field goal record with a forty-yard kick. *The Sporting News* declared Jack Jones Coach of the Year.

In November 1990, sophomore Kim Gardner won the Missouri Class-4A girls' track finals, a first for the high school, with a time of 19 minutes and 39 seconds in the 5k run. Two years later, she became a three-time state champion after winning in cross country as well as in the 800m and 1500m races.

Track star Robert Newberry, Class of 1992, earned nearly thirty gold medals during his four-year high school career. He broke the state record twice, with a time of 14.02, a record standing for twenty years, which had been set by high school alumnus James Bell.

Two Statesmen wrestlers won state championships in February 1991. Charles White took first place in the 140 pound weight class, and Tommy Killian won first place in the 114-pound category. Both

Saturday morning practices prepared Judo Club members for meets and progression through belt colors.

wrestlers went undefeated. High school varsity wrestling coach Carl Stallings produced over thirty-five state champions, including Steve Fantroy, Class of 1992, and Marlowe Parsons, Class of 1993.

On the health front, the high school's smokers' days were numbered. The School Board declared a "smoke-free environment" by the fall of 1991, and the ban applied to staff, students, and campus visitors.

Vintage clothing became one way for students to express their individuality. Many students scoured Goodwill, Amvets, the Scholarshop, the New Hope, and other charity organizations for coats, hats, dresses, formals, and jewelry to recycle while contributing to worthwhile causes.

Academic standards tightened. The State Education Department required achievement testing. State universities scrutinized class rank and ACT/SAT scores. Since the fall of 1989, the Missouri High School Activities Association required student athletes to pass a minimum of five classes each semester. Weighted grades rewarded students taking honors courses with higher grade-point averages.

The Top Hat Awards, introduced in May 1991, lauded exemplary students. Any high school staff member could nominate a "Top Hat" student, who was presented with an engraved medallion. The ceremony followed a continental breakfast catered by Old Orchard's McDonald's, a local Renaissance business supporter.

Promising minority students supplemented their education in weekend and summer programs such as the Upward Bound Program at Saint Louis University and the national Inroads Program through Washington University, Saint Louis University, and the University of Missouri. Guidance counselor Lillian Curtis facilitated the Inroads Program in recruiting Hispanic, African American, Native American, and other high school students for communications, management, and leadership training for corporate America. Juniors in good standing and maintaining a 3.0 GPA or ranking in the top 10 percent of their class were eligible for the program.

Pegasus, the high school's gifted program, used students' math and verbal scores and teacher recommendations to provide accelerated English classes. Seniors were offered internships in a special field of interest under the supervision of a faculty mentor.

The Metropolitan Student Leadership Program (MSLP) trained faculty-nominated student representatives in leadership skills. Ten high school juniors and a faculty sponsor participated in team-building and problem-solving activities along with students and sponsors from eighteen St. Louis area schools.

The 1988 state championship team was built on a strong running game and stingy defense.

Coach Stallings' "grapplers" claim another victory.

Skateboards, a 1980s craze, found the courtyard an appealing place to demonstrate one's skills.

A plainclothes policeman joined the high school staff in the fall of 1991. Although high school principal Jerry Knight had established a Police Department/High School Partnership in the 1970s, for the first time, a full-time police resource officer maintained an office in the building. Emphasis remained on crime prevention and counseling, while onsite community policing allowed for the investigation of thefts, assaults, vandalism, and substance abuse. The high school's program became a national model in police-school cooperation.

In February 1991, Dr. Edwards announced a full-scholarship opportunity for four-year Renaissance gold cardholders. Northeast Missouri State University President Russell Warren offered free tuition, room, and board to Webster Groves High School graduates maintaining a 4. 0 grade-point average for four years of high school.

The district recommitted itself to its full spectrum of students. At its October 21, 1991, meeting, the School Board pledged "to continue and improve programs for low-achieving students, to give students the right to choose and explore, and to stay aware that the district is committed to its diverse student population."

High school English teachers Agnes Gregg, Minnie Phillips, Theresa Wojak, Beth Ann Brady, Carrie Henly, and Chestra Peaslee joined Hixson Middle School English teachers in the Webster Groves Writing Project. The voluntary action research team worked to improve student writing by focusing on low-achieving African American students. The group described their experiences, teaching

Each staff member is permitted to nominate and present a Top Hat Award to one student each year in a special assembly.

strategies, and action-research results in two books: *Hear You, Hear Me: Lessons from the Webster Groves Writing Project*, published by the Webster Groves School District through a U.S. Department of Education Innovation grant in 1992, and *Mirror Images: Teaching Writing in Black and White*, published by Heinemann in 1994.

Science teacher Larry Horak used cooperative learning and student teams in heterogeneous biology classes. The high school continued its practice of assigning strong teachers to students in basic-level classes.

The high school's "Wall of Fame" was unveiled in January 1992. Dr. Edwards commissioned art teacher Lee Drake to design the wall to recognize distinguished high school alumni and to inspire current students. Honorees were nominated and selected based on demonstrated excellence in their fields and/or their contributions to society over an extended period of time.

The high school's music program gathered new strength through its March "Music in Our School" (MIOS) program. As part of a national initiative, the high school band and vocal music concerts throughout the district's schools and community provided an opportunity for students, teachers, parents, and citizens to participate.

Physical education attained academic stature in the summer of 1992, when the required course

The Webster Groves juvenile officers assisted with campus happenings.

was figured into grade-point averages. Physical education teacher Gloria Smith stated, "Physical education is a requirement and should be treated like the other required courses. We have written and skill tests. We offer a sound course."

Coffee cup in hand, Dan Edwards daily greeted students at the senior entrance and repeated the ritual as they departed for home. During his leadership, every high school student was entitled a voice. Under his policy of inclusion, voluntary transfer students contributed mightily to the high school's athletic championships, cultural diversity, and scholarship awards. When Dr. Edwards resigned as principal in 1992, he left assured that he had helped to restore the school pride of "some of the finest students in the nation."

Yvonne Kauffman

"Academic excellence thrives at WGHS," declared the *Echo* newspaper on its January 1993 cover, and by all appearances the high school's 1980s slump was over. Yet, signs pointed to an achievement gap that would worry the high school in coming decades.

The administration and faculty responded with an array of innovations: curriculum pilots, freshmen unit restructuring, smaller classes for basic learners, alternative scheduling, and a mentoring program. Yvonne "Vonnie" Kauffman, the high school's seventh principal, led the effort to produce widespread achievement.

Ms. Kauffman arrived at the high school in July 1992, as an administrator in the Jemez Valley School District near Albuquerque, New Mexico. At Webster Groves High School, she adopted a personalized counseling approach, encouraging students to improve grade-point averages, to take better care of the building, and to become involved in volunteer service projects.

Then-Assistant Principal Pat Voss organized a "task force" of students in January 1993 to improve school-community relations as well as the community's image of high school students. "Whatever we do, we must do it well," she told the nineteen student volunteers from every grade level.

The group set four goals: 1) volunteering time and talent to keep the community abreast of what was going on at the high school; 2) investigating recreational opportunities for students needing constructive outlets; 3) establishing communication with households without children in the schools to keep them informed of what is happening in the school; and 4) reaching out to families with children in private or parochial schools to improve their perceptions of Webster Groves High School.

The high school marked its tenth anniversary in the Voluntary Transfer Student Program in the fall of 1993. The district had enrolled a total of 3,100 transfer students since the plan's inception in 1983, and transfer students accounted for 10 percent of the district's population. Of the high school's 1,279 enrollment, voluntary students numbered 118, most saying they participated in the program because it afforded them a better education than their resident schools.

Pilot School, a new alternative program, opened in the annex in the fall of 1993, with forty-two nontraditional learners and students performing below grade level. Social studies teacher Kim Buckey implemented the program, along with outdoor education teacher David Cady and Special

A change of venue found the spring "meller-dramer" unfolding in the snack bar.

Yvonne Kauffman assumed leadership of WGHS in the fall of 1992, staying only two years before returning to New Mexico.

Out with the old, in the with new, as a bond issue provided new classroom furniture.

School District teacher Roxanne Devine. The three-hour interdisciplinary course combined science, history, English, and practical arts in a study of St. Louis history, science, and technology. Students spent the remainder of the school day in regular classes.

English teacher Carrie Henly introduced Continents and Cultures, a two-hour interdisciplinary course for tenth graders, in the fall of 1993. The course enrolled 160 students, and English and social studies teaching teams offered a thematic approach to studying politics, economics, social structure, aesthetic and media interpretation, language, and communication. Teachers used problem-solving, critical thinking, and research skills in small and large group interaction to explore relationships among traditionally separate subjects.

The English Department moved to portfolio evaluation of its writing program. Students selected writing samples based on four criteria: variety and versatility, craft and care, beauty and power, and thoughtful reflection. The goal was to track student writing growth from grades 6 through 12 through formal and informal assessment.

When Yvonne Kauffman returned to New Mexico in the fall of 1994, she left Webster Groves High School in the hands of three assistant principals. One of them, Pat Voss, became the high school's eighth principal.

Senior year concluded with a ride on a paddleboat at Lake Holiday as part of class day.

Chapter 8

> *"First and foremost, I am and always will be a teacher. My goal has always been to help kids grow academically and personally."*
>
> —Pat Voss

She knew the school. She knew the students. She knew the parents and the community. She had served as the unofficial dean of student council, senior prom, and graduation. Now, after rising through the ranks as social studies teacher, activities director, assistant principal, and interim principal, Patricia Voss became the high school's eighth principal.

Pat Voss came to the high school in the fall of 1969, four years after teaching social studies at Rosati-Kain, a private Catholic girls' high school in St. Louis City. She held bachelor and master's degrees in social studies and history from Central Missouri State University in Warrensburg and a second master's degree in educational administration from the University of Missouri–St. Louis.

At Webster Groves High School, her strong teaching, organizational, and leadership skills earned the respect of her colleagues and principal Jerry Knight, who appointed her director of student activities in 1974 and chair of the North Central Association evaluation visits in 1982–83 and 1989–90. After serving as interim principal in the fall of 1994, she was appointed principal in 1995.

Ms. Voss continued restructuring of the high school program begun under Dan Edwards in the 1980s and encouraged by her predecessor, Yvonne Kauffman, in the early 1990s. The seven-period rotating schedule, implemented in 1994, allowed students to take additional courses and to accumulate more graduation credits, resulting in an increase in course offerings, extracurricular activities, and student participation.

A new outdoor club offered day and weekend trips for hiking, caving, camping, and orienteering. Sponsors Bob Chekoudjian, David Cady, and Marty Walter led bimonthly trips to Rockwood Reservation, Meramec State Park, Greensfelder County Park, and Silver Mines.

In the fall of 1995, the new Senior Leadership Seminar offered training in practical and everyday leadership skills. David Cady taught the three-hour course for credit in history, psychology, and physical education. The class included field trips, guest speakers, research, current events, class projects, community service, and reading assignments. Mr. Cady also planned urban adventures, orienteering, rock climbing, rappelling, and other outdoor activities for survival training and team-building.

Always up for a challenge, Pat Voss rode her motorcycle to and from WGHS.

facing page: The 1998–99 cross country team poses with the hardware won at meets throughout the season.

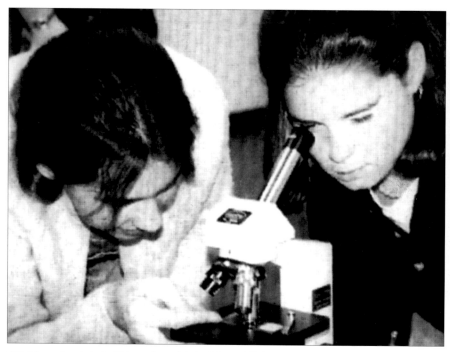

Betsy Moppert, a student-athlete, analyzes data for Advanced Biology.

The pressure was on to get hooked up correctly, as Molly Copper prepared to rappel from the roof of Roberts Gym.

The athletics program issued student contracts in the winter of 1995. Athletes agreed to refrain from smoking, drugs, and alcohol while playing sports and to project a positive image as representatives of the school. Cheerleaders and Guard/Danceline also signed contracts.

A new weightlifting class grew in popularity. "Students have really responded to work under a professional weight trainer and to having someone push them through the process," said physical education teacher and fitness coach Ken Manwarring. During the offseason, athletes used the program and facilities for physical conditioning.

Senior Michelle Kelley became the high school's first female hockey player when she joined the junior varsity team in the fall of 1994. After moving from Texas in her freshman year, Michelle became interested in hockey, learned to skate, and took a few camps during her sophomore year. Coach Dave Garth commented, "She's a natural athlete and a better skater than many of the guys on the team."

Betsey Moppert, the following year, became the kicker for the boys' freshmen football team. She completed nine out of ten attempts, earning her the respect of her team. "No one seems to care that she's a girl," said teammate Kevin Nordmann.

The boys' lacrosse team gained varsity status in 1996. The team played Kirkwood, DeSmet, Lafayette, Parkway North, Ladue, Hazelwood Central, Saint Louis University High School, and Country Day School. Sean Shubert coached the team, and high school alumnus James McGill served as assistant coach. Home games were played at Steger Field.

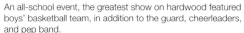

An all-school event, the greatest show on hardwood featured boys' basketball team, in addition to the guard, cheerleaders, and pep band.

Johnnie Parker dominates his opponent for another two points.

"March Madness" erupted when the varsity boys' basketball team won the Missouri State Class 4A championship in Columbia on March 9, 1996. After beating Independence's Truman High School 54–51 in the semifinals, the Statesmen defeated the West Plains Zizzers 54–53 for the state title.

"School was basically called off for the state game," senior Katie Stokes told *Echo* reporter Megan Lockett. "Everyone went [to the basketball game] and we were so spirited. I will never forget the awesome feeling when I looked around and all I could see was orange and black."

The 1996 "Dream Team" and future 2006 Webster Groves High School Sports Hall of Famers consisted of Dan Wacker, Tate Decker, Sam Snelling, Matt Caldwell, Johnnie Parker, Spencer Taylor, David Brader, Brett Buresch, John Marecek, Latrelle Yancey, Rick Ewing, Stephen Rhodes, Eddie Hester, and Travis Brown. Tim Moore was proclaimed "Coach of the Year."

Moore had come to the high school in 1984, with teaching and coaching experience spanning from St. Paul's High School in Louisiana to Country Day School (now MICDS) in St. Louis County. Like the legendary Charlie Roberts over fifty years before, Moore taught mathematics and considered himself a teacher instead of a coach. His goal was not to produce superstars but student-athletes who learned how to use their time wisely. His teams won regional titles in Illinois and district sectional titles in Missouri. Moore was inducted into the Missouri Basketball Coaches Association (MBCA) Hall of Fame in 2005.

Jocelyn Grant, Class of 1996, and President Bill Clinton enjoy some informal time following the presentation in Roberts Gym.

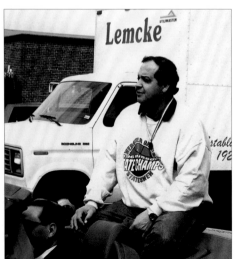

Tim Moore, Missouri State Basketball Coach of the Year, accepts congratulations from the crowd as he rides in the victory parade.

The high school's euphoria lasted through the spring of 1996 and surged anew when Pat Voss announced that President Bill Clinton would visit the high school on Friday, May 17. In a nationally televised speech, the president commended the high school on its drug and violence prevention program, coordinated by Assistant Principal John Raimondo. Ms. Voss was "assisted" by the White House Secret Service with making arrangements but stood firmly on one condition: every high school student would be permitted to attend the speech in Roberts Gym.

The capacity crowd reached 1,700, counting high school students, community leaders, St. Louis–area and state politicians, district administrators, elementary student representatives, and parent volunteers. President Clinton entered the gymnasium at 1:45 p.m., and Pat Voss welcomed guests. Missouri Congressman Dick Gephardt made preliminary remarks. High school senior Jocelyn Grant spoke on behalf of the student body. The president, in his keynote address, implored students to strive for a free and peaceful world.

Special Olympics became the high school's community service project. The Moss Field contests had begun with sponsors and volunteers from clubs, sports teams, and other organizations. Eventually, the competitions evolved into a junior class project, with high school "buddies" cheering on disabled athletes ages six through twenty-two in running, jumping, and throwing contests in a mutually rewarding day.

Buddy and athlete get "psyched" as the race approaches at the Special Olympics.

Meanwhile, the arts quietly flourished. Teacher and professional ceramics artist Karen Antrim nurtured student artists and apprentices in her "workshop" in Room 202. The Kirkwood native had spent twenty-one years teaching art in Cedar Rapids, Iowa, before coming to WGHS in 1993. Her most promising (and even reluctant) students excelled in traditional, modern, and whimsical pottery and sculpture. "I love it when they get involved in their artwork, even if they don't plan to go to art school," commented Antrim.

The high school, along with its neighbor Webster University, established a "Cooperative Partnership" in the fall of 1997 to share facilities and resources. In an effort to alleviate overcrowding in its night classes, the university rented classroom space at the high school and purchased new chairs, tables, air-conditioning, whiteboards, mounted VCRs, and computers for high school use during the school day. Also, the university opened its facilities to the high school for district staff meetings, workshops, staff-student-faculty retreats, and emergency shelter in the event of a crisis.

The state monitored school and student performance with the implementation of the Missouri Assessment Program (MAP) in the spring of 1997. The standardized testing program stemmed from the Outstanding Schools Act of 1993, prompting the Missouri State Board of Education to direct the Department of Elementary and Secondary Education (DESE) to identify key competencies that Missouri students should demonstrate before graduation. The seventy-three Show-Me Standards

At the potters wheel, clay and talented hands begin the process of creating a work of art.

The girls try their hands at a little jazz improvisation.

Time photographer Steve Liss takes the time to get up close and personal with the students of WGHS.

required a solid foundation in core subject areas and application of knowledge and skills in real-world, everyday contexts. Each spring, sophomores were tested in mathematics and science, and juniors were assessed in communication arts and social studies. The state used its assessment program to standardize curriculum across the state, measure school and student progress, and to determine a district's accreditation status.

A-Men, the high school's all-male a cappella group, debuted in the spring of 1998. Math teacher Eric Dunn formed the group, after singing in and directing a similar group in college. Dunn thought that performing pop standards such as Jimmy Cliff's "I Can See Clearly," Simon and Garfunkel's "Cecelia," and Boyz to Men's "It's So Hard to Say Goodbye to Yesterday" celebrated vocal music, built student confidence, and galvanized school spirit. He recruited, auditioned, rehearsed, and led fifteen young men in a "rite of passage" at assemblies and concerts drawing a near-cult following.

The Music Department's jazz bands made their third pilgrimage to New Orleans' French Quarter Music Festival in April 1995. After the thirteen-hour bus trip, students fine-tuned their skills amid the "pleasurable distraction" of the music, food, and people of pre-Hurricane Katrina New Orleans.

Time Magazine reporters arrived at the high school in the fall of 1999, in the national media's seemingly perpetual search for the "typical American teenager" in the "typical American high school." The magazine's September 27–October 1, 1999, edition resembled its 1998 cover story, "A Week in the Life of a Hospital."

During the first two weeks of September, reporters and photographers "shadowed" students around school, at home, and in the community. They attended classes, club meetings, and extracurricular events. They held morning magazine meetings and deciphered notes in local coffeehouses. They interviewed students, staff, and parents for the forty-page article on school clubs, sports, classes, and issues interspersed with student and faculty cameos.

November 2000, the Frisco Bell is lifted in celebration of a long-awaited Turkey Day win by the Statesmen.

Stephanie Bergheger, Class of 2002, offered her view of *Time's* "investigation" for a high school *Echo* reporter: "There is no such thing as the average high school since each high school is different."

The high school's new dress code, in 1999, required a semblance of uniformity. There were no hats or headgear worn in school. There were no "saggin'" or "baggin'" pants, no midriff blouses, and no barebacked shirts. There were no pagers, gang-related clothing or symbols, and no clothing or jewelry displaying sexual content, drugs, alcohol, violence, or obscene language. Students responded by wearing trendy clothing and "anti-fashion" tee-shirts.

Subcultures resurfaced at the high school in 1998, most prominent among them "Gothic" or "Goth," "Punk," "Straight Edge," and "Skaters." "Goths" donned black attire and makeup displaying their individuality and open-mindedness. "Punks" commingled lifestyle and music. "Straight Edgers" pledged "clean living," with no-drugs, no-smoking, and no-alcohol. Some "Straight Edgers" were vegetarians, vegans, and avowed celibates. Free-spirited "Skaters" remained devotees of rollerblading and skateboarding.

The high school became a fully designated "A+ School" in 1999, providing an opportunity for graduates to receive state benefits for their college education. Then-Assistant Principal Jon Clark had spearheaded efforts in the 1996–97 school year, resulting in the high school becoming one of ten county schools to be chosen for the program. "A+ students" were required to maintain a 2.5 grade-point average, a 95 percent attendance rate, to complete fifty hours of community service, and to display a record of good citizenship. Graduates were then eligible for free tuition and books for any public community college or technical school in Missouri.

The year 2000 ushered in plans for a new state-of-the-art high school cafeteria, the end of open campus, and the return of the Frisco Bell. Passage of a $10 million district bond issue authorized $3 million for high school renovations, most of which was used for a modern cafeteria. Restaurant-style kitchen equipment replaced appliances dating back to the 1930s and 1940s. Round eating tables, booths, and lighting provided a student-friendly climate. A snack bar area and cafeteria service lines offered a smorgasbord of menu options resembling a commercial food court.

The air-conditioned cafeteria opened in the fall of 2001, while School Board policy restricted students to the campus. Only seniors during lunch and students at off-campus learning stations were accorded off-campus privileges.

After a three-year absence, the Frisco Bell returned to the high school when the varsity football team defeated Kirkwood 31–9 at Moss Field on November 21, 2000. Kurt Odenwald was the winning quarterback, and linebacker Derrick Ming and center Lennie Harris were standouts. Cliff Ice was the winning coach. The team's season record stood at 7–3.

The Skatesmen hockey team celebrated a winning tradition. After nine Turkey Day victories, including a 9–3 win in 2000, the Skatesmen emerged with one of its strongest teams in the fall of 2001. Dave Garth coached the team, senior goalie Russ Sprague was a four-year veteran, and junior goaltender Jon Edwards was steadily progressing. Since the Skatesmen were not a state-sanctioned school sports organization, high school football coach Cliff Ice sponsored the team to support the team's enthusiasm, talent, sportsmanship, and hard work.

WGHS stages a Comedy Sports Assembly for the student body.

Women, Gender, and Diversity AP became part of the high school curriculum in the fall of 2001. English teacher Kristin Moore, holding a master's degree in Interdisciplinary Women's Studies, taught the class to juniors and seniors. The course offered advanced readings and open discussion focusing on cultural, political, and historical issues pertaining to women. Students could opt to pay tuition for college credit through the University of Missouri–St. Louis.

Circle of Friends, a support group for socially disabled students, organized in February 2001. Student volunteers welcomed ninth graders and ate lunch with students outside their social circles. The group also helped special needs students in the classroom and participated in conflict mediation to ease tensions throughout the school.

Senior and junior volunteers continued the tradition of serving as camp counselors for the school district's fifth graders. Elementary fifth-grade classes took turns in April or May, spending a week at Camp Wyman in Eureka, Missouri. Counselors and campers participated in outdoor activities and environmental studies.

Assistant Principal George White won the Council on Disabilities Inclusion Award's "Educator of the Year" in October 2001, in recognition of his pioneering work on behalf of children with disabilities. Dr. White welcomed and supported educational opportunities for handicapped students at the high school and by 2003 was honored as Missouri Assistant Principal of the Year.

Improvisational theatre took center stage at the school's annual Comedy Sports Assembly. Drama teacher Ed Grooms began the event in 1998, and by January 2002, teacher and student audiences awaited the competitions to ease the winter doldrums. Comedy sports spread to nationwide improvisation competitions to determine which groups would represent drama classes while sharpening participants' improvisational skills.

The 2002–03 school year brought a change in student government. Student Council (StuCo) replaced the Student Legislative Board (SLB) to provoke more student involvement, more success for each class, and better interclass communication. The Student Service Council (SSC) was renamed Class Council. StuCo focused on service projects and student activities. Class Council representation was elected in school assemblies after campaigns by candidates. StuCo elections were held during lunch or in the office instead of at an assembly. Both organizations sought wider student input and participation.

The Statesmen 2002 football season ended with a whimper *and* a bang: sacrifice of the Frisco Bell for a state championship. *Sports Illustrated's* Mark Bowden, former Webster Groves resident and author of the 1999 best-seller *Black Hawk Down: A Story of Modern War*, chronicled the 87th Turkey Day game for the magazine's December 9, 2002, edition. Instead of the traditional varsity slugfest, Bowden found a smaller-scale, though-no-less-pugnacious contest between the two schools' freshmen and sophomore junior varsity teams at Moss Field on November 28.

Bowden heard the story of how, in 1988 when the Turkey Day game was cancelled because Webster Groves High School went to state, school officials from both schools agreed that in the event that either or both of them advanced to the playoffs, they would substitute their JV teams to continue the rivalry in unbroken succession. Now, on November 23, 2002, after defeating McCluer North 39–38 in the semifinals, the Statesmen varsity football team was in just such a place.

While the JV team lost to Kirkwood 28–14, the Statesmen varsity team prevailed after beating Kansas City–area's Raymore-Peculiar High School 23–22, on November 30 at the Edward Jones Dome in downtown St. Louis, for the state 5A title.

The end of the school year marked the end of an era for Pat Voss. On June 6, 2003, the student commons was named the Patricia Voss (P.V.) Student Commons, "in grateful appreciation for her dedication to the students of Webster Groves High School, 1969–2003." Pat Voss would continue her service to the district, as she had for thirty-three years, this time as director of the district's alumni association.

The Statesmen capture their third state football championship.

Chapter 9

> *"We cannot rest on our laurels; we must consider new ideas, approaches, perspectives, and ways to be more effective with and for our students. If we are comfortable with being a good school, we will never challenge ourselves to become a great school. Stepping outside of our comfort zones is not easy but essential for growth."*
>
> —Jon Clark

Competition, according to Jon Clark, was a good thing. The former college basketball player and mathematics teacher not only wanted his students to become winners in the county, contenders in the state, but also all-star champions. Every staff member would coach the squad, and every student would get playing time. Webster Groves High School would become his team.

Dr. Clark was lucky enough to get himself born into a family of educators. Growing up on a farm outside St. Joseph, Missouri, he watched his parents rise at 4 a.m. to complete chores. Both parents were career teachers. His father also coached basketball and worked in the administration building. His older sister became a kindergarten teacher, and his younger sister, according to him, was "the best elementary physical education teacher in Missouri." Since his earliest recollections, *hardworking* and *best* became prerequisites for educational success.

After attending Northwest Missouri State University in Maryville on a four-year basketball and academic scholarship and graduating with bachelor and master's degrees in mathematics education, Jon Clark taught math and coached varsity basketball for two years at John F. Hodge High School in St. James, Missouri, and for five years in Rolla. In Rolla, he met then-Superintendent D. Kent King, later Missouri's commissioner of Elementary and Secondary Education, who encouraged him to pursue a career in school administration.

While working toward a doctoral degree at Saint Louis University, Clark's teacher, Dr. William P. Gussner, then-superintendent of Webster Groves School District, informed him of an opening at the high school for assistant principal. Although Clark planned on returning to Rolla, King cited Webster Groves' long-standing educational reputation and Clark's potential for professional growth. So Jon Clark arrived at Webster Groves High School in the summer of 1996 and eventually succeeded Pat Voss as principal in 2003.

Dr. Jon Clark experiences the joy of awarding a diploma to a member of the Class of 2005.

facing page: Ben Walker and Becca Hughes show their school spirit.

The Cat in the Hat and friends visit WGHS during the run of *Seussical the Musical.*

Turkey Day became his "real initiation." He fell in love with the suburb's sense of tradition and small-town community within a big city. While the students were allowed more freedom than he was accustomed to, a mutual respect existed between students and teachers, who were committed to helping students beyond the classroom. Dr. Clark used his seven years as assistant principal to build relationships with staff and students.

Seussical: The Musical debuted at the high school in November 2005, five years after opening on Broadway. Courtney Lewis starred as the Cat in the Hat, Kate Lilly as JoJo (Boy), Ben Walker as Horton the Elephant, and Mandy Radick as Gertrude McFuzz in Lynn Ahrens and Stephen Flaherty's witty compilation of Dr. Seuss's books, characters, and lessons about friendship, perseverance, human dignity, natural beauty, peaceful coexistence, and the power of imagination. Director and high school drama teacher Sarah Romanowski said that she chose the show because "I have so much talent this year, and the show features many actors and actresses." Scott Kinworthy served as music director, and for the first time, the Drama and Music Departments offered a Saturday matinee in addition to evening performances.

With a level western Missouri accent, Dr. Clark "spoke from the heart." He strove for the success of every student through academic programs, activities, clubs, sports, and scholarships. He strengthened the transition from middle school to high school for incoming freshmen. He wrote grants for staff development, technology, student tutoring, scholarship assistance, and student leadership. He recruited students for ACT test review classes. He attended after-school events, celebrations, and ceremonies for students and staff alike. He fostered stronger communication between faculty and parents. He worked relentlessly to reduce the academic achievement gap between African American and Caucasian students. He led by example.

Since 1996, the high school had maintained solid levels of achievement, with the majority of students taking challenging courses. Many enrolled in college-credit classes. Over 80 percent planned to attend two- or four-year colleges. Yet despite shifting demographics, the "above-average" standard of achievement required rethinking. The aim was 100 percent.

In 1996–97, the A+ Schools Program was implemented to motivate "average" and "above-average"

Where do I want to go to college? Check out the College Fair and do some comparative shopping.

students. The Missouri grant-sponsored program sought to reduce the dropout rate, to increase career awareness, and to provide tuition for eligible students enrolling in community colleges.

Dr. Clark enlisted the services of the Guidance Department to play a more active role in student planning. The annual College Night served as the centerpiece for informing students and parents about the career and college search process. Counselors targeted juniors and shared information about SAT and ACT tests, the A+ Schools Program, and Advanced Placement exams. For seniors, they shared tips for writing college essays and applying for financial aid. College representatives set up information booths and followed with school visits. An after-school ACT review class offered test-taking strategies. Counselors also visited classrooms to introduce themselves to freshmen and to prepare sophomores for the Preliminary American College Test (PLAN) to guide high school preparation for college and/or career paths.

By the fall of 2006, the high school had reason to celebrate. Scores on the Advanced Placement Test (AP), Scholastic Aptitude Test (SAT), and American College Test (ACT) were the highest in the school's history. Yet the achievement gap persisted between African American and Caucasian students. "The gap didn't emerge overnight, so it won't disappear overnight," Dr. Clark admitted. Yet he remained adamant in making progress.

Career Day expanded to eighty volunteer speakers, sharing information and experiences about occupations ranging from television anchor to master chef. A bi-annual event, the sessions fell under

Mr. Wojak helps his advanced physics students with an experiment.

the supervision of the A+ Schools Program coordinator beginning in 1997. After surveying student interests and matching interests to volunteers, the school offered students the opportunity to learn about careers, sample the job market, and ask questions in three different career sessions.

The Statesmen Service Award recognized the contributions of students with 50+, 100+, or 200+ volunteer service hours. Students in the A+ Schools Program were required to complete at least fifty hours of tutoring and mentoring, and many students volunteered in school service organizations or worked with youth or mission groups. For years, KUTO (Kids Under Twenty-One) drew student volunteers for its suicide prevention hotline. Church youth groups also assisted disadvantaged families during spring break or worked with disadvantaged kids at summer camps. The James T. Hixson Service Award recognized the school service of graduating seniors.

Fall and spring parent-teacher conferences, implemented under Pat Voss in the spring of 1997, strengthened the communication between teachers and parents. Dr. Clark later urged teachers to invite parents to the conferences who would benefit most from teacher-parent contact. The internet also improved school communication. Homework web pages allowed students, parents, and tutors to check assignments, and e-mail made it easier and convenient for parents to check student progress.

Weighted grades in honors classes were reviewed. Initiated in 1987, the 5-point scale grades, some faculty members felt, led to grade inflation or the race to take weighted courses to improve class rank and one's grade-point average. Many colleges refigured weighted grades on a 4-point scale, while non-weighted high school classrooms experienced the flight of highly motivated students. Faculty consensus was to reduce the 5-point scale to 4.5, compared to 4.0 for students in non-weighted classes.

The Family and Consumer Science (FACS) students prepare sack lunches for the homeless.

A quarter-of-a-million-dollar grant helps the high school stay current with technology.

Graduation requirements rose from twenty-two credits to twenty-four, beginning with the incoming freshmen Class of 2008. When the high school moved to a seven-period schedule in 1994, students typically earned more credits than they needed, resulting in laxity during their senior year. A high school graduation committee, led by Jon Clark while assistant principal, recommended raising credits to maximize student learning over four years of high school. The requirements also included a half-credit technology course and additional elective. Effective for the Class of 2010, the Missouri State Board of Education raised credit requirements for specific subject areas—to four years of English, three years of social studies, three years of mathematics, three years of science, and one-half credit of personal finance.

Dual-credit courses made the transition from high school to college smoother for some students. The University of Missouri–St. Louis and Saint Louis University offered college credit for honors courses ranging from art history, advanced foreign language classes, advanced physics, honors U.S. studies, to women, gender, and diversity. St. Louis Community College offered articulated credit for selected courses in business, college English, and college algebra.

Given the pervasiveness of technology, the high school Business Department expanded its computer courses. Classes such as multimedia and design literacy, desktop publishing, web design, computer applications, and introduction to networking literacy were open to all students. CISCO Certified Networking equipped juniors and seniors in networking basics, routers, and routing while offering articulated credit through St. Louis Community College.

Students as Allies, like the Committee of Forty under Dan Edwards in the late 1980s, helped to

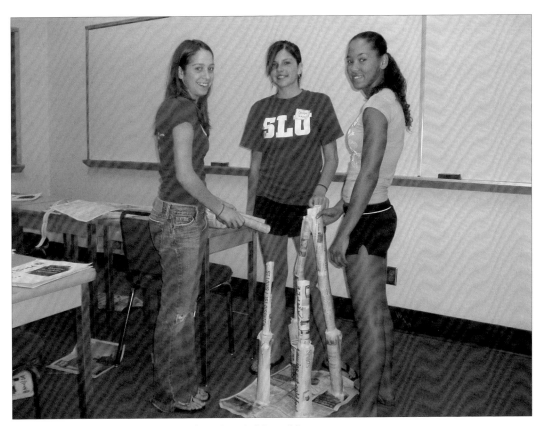

Participants in the Future Leaders program work on a team-building activity.

improve communication among students, the administration, and the faculty. With support from a grant from the MetLife Foundation in the 2003, Webster Groves High School worked independently along with five regional high schools (Francis Howell Central, Wentzville Holt, Lindbergh, Perryville, and Rockwood Summit) to develop a local action plan to create a high school environment with mutual respect among teachers and students.

GSA (Gay-Straight Alliance), a student support group, organized in the 2003–04 school year to reinforce the school's nondiscrimination guidelines. The club formed after the murder of Matthew Shepard, a gay college student in Wyoming, in a local effort to promote tolerance and to create a safe school environment regardless of sexual orientation. The administration strengthened its stance on discipline to read: "Sexual harassment of students by employees or other students of the opposite or same sex is strictly prohibited. Students are expected to report any act of violence or harassment to a principal or other staff member."

The varsity Statesmen basketball team continued its winning tradition with thirty-eight consecutive conference victories from 2002 through 2006, while reigning as Suburban South Conference Champions. Under Head Coach Jay Blossom, the team played one of the most rigorous schedules

The 2006 varsity men's basketball Statesmen send holiday greetings.

in the state, including the Bass Pro Tournament of Champions in Springfield, Missouri; Marshall County's Hoopfest in Benton, Kentucky; the Gatorade Timberwolves Shootout in Minneapolis; the Massac County Shootout in Massac, Illinois; and the KMOX Shootout and the Pioneer Bank-Webster Classic in St. Louis.

Following a dry spell of state championships, the high school celebrated two star athletes in May 2006: Jenna Harris in swimming and Geoffrey Daniel in track. Having set the state record of 1 minute and 50.40 seconds for the 200-yard freestyle, Jenna won both the 200- and 500-yard freestyle in 2006. She was voted the high school's swimming MVP, All-Metro Swimmer of the Year, and All-American by the National Interscholastic Swim Coaches Association (NISCA) for her 200 and 500 individual events and the 200 and 400 freestyle relays. Her coach, Dan Broshears, was named Coach of the Year. In track, Geoffrey Daniel's triple jump of 46-10 earned him the Class 4 title and the high school's first state track championship since Tim Rusan, two-time state champion and national triple jumper, won in 1995. Dan Sebben coached both Daniel and Rusan.

During spring break, in April 2005, the high school band flew to Prague for the "ultimate field trip," according to band teacher Jackie Stillwell. The band had become seasoned travelers, journeying to England twice and to New Orleans at least six times before Hurricane Katrina devastated the city in

The band students peek from the columns of a spa in Karlovy Vary on their trip to the Czech Republic.

August 2005. The trip to the Czech Republic set a precedent: combining musical performances with a cultural tour. Band students made Czech friends, visited castles, took winding bus tours through bucolic hillside towns, sampled McDonald's and Beatles music Czech-style, and performed before 400 students at the Gymnasium Liben, one of the top high schools in Prague. They added to their itinerary a performance at the Czech-Anglo High School in the southern Bohemian town of Ceske Budejovice.

The choir's turn came the following year, when in April 2006 they traveled to New York City, where they earned first and second place at the Heritage Festival. Directed by Scott Kinworthy, the Concert Choir and women's choirs ranked first out of forty-eight schools performing at Riverside Church. Chamber Choir ranked second. Overall, the choirs tied with Rancho Verde and Greece Arcadia high schools for first place. Eighty-six students and sixteen chaperones made the sixteen-hour bus trip to New York City.

Jon Clark was selected as the St. Louis Association of Secondary Schools Principal of the Year in 2005. He was too busy to celebrate. Instead, he focused on a collaborative effort by staff, students, parents, and the community for school improvement. Student needs came first. The key, he believed, lay in student involvement, communication, and empowerment through shared decision-making. He valued feedback by modeling feedback. He met yearly with small groups of students, tenth graders in the fall and eleventh graders in the spring, to listen to student views about the school. He made students an integral part of faculty and staff interviews and presenters at school board meetings. Students also completed teacher surveys to improve classroom instruction.

After launching the Statesmen Center in the 2006–07, Dr. Clark realized another of his dreams. He had supervised an alternative program in Rolla and believed that an individualized learning and credit-recovery center within the high school would allow for a more flexible curriculum, create more opportunities for student success, and reduce the dropout rate. Students would spend part of their day in the regular school program and would remain eligible to participate in extracurricular activities.

Phase I had brought major remodeling of the cafeteria and the PV Commons in the year 2000. Passage of an unprecedented no-tax-increase $40 million bond issue, Proposition V, in April 2006 ensured continuation of the district's ten-year scheduled renovations. Phase II found installation of central air conditioning in all district buildings at a cost of $19 million. In addition, this phase focused on high school improvements, including a new floor, lighting, technology, and acoustic upgrades for the sixty-year-old Roberts Gym (completed ahead of schedule in the fall of 2006), a new competition gym, and new locker rooms. Preparation for central air conditioning for the entire high school began the summer of 2007.

Jon Clark set renovation priorities by consulting the faculty, student groups, parents, and his community advisory council. Future planning, for Phase III, includes technology improvement throughout the building. Most importantly, faculty requests for flexible classroom space and learning labs seemed to indicate that the search for "new approaches" to moving Webster Groves High School from a good school to a great school was well under way.

The Riverside Cathedral in New York City was the scene of the Concert Choir's April 2006 performance.

Chapter 10

> *"Whatever the purpose of high school was in former times it is now declared to be the training of our youth to make the best adjustment to the ever-changing programs of society."*
> —James T. Hixson

What Webster Groves School District Superintendent W. D. Grove called the "People's College" in 1909 today is a far cry from the six-room high school the district dedicated in the spring of 1905 and opened in the fall of 1907. The district now includes five communities: Webster Groves, Rock Hill, Shrewsbury, Warson Woods, and Glendale, as well as tuition-paying families. Also the re-renovated three-story high school campus spans nearly one block between Lockwood and Bradford avenues.

The 1907 classical and scientific curriculum has expanded to over 200 courses, including Computer Networking, Japanese, Outdoor Education, Military History, Personal Finance, Women and Gender Studies, and Modern International Literature. The faculty of six, including the principal, now numbers over 100, and the graduating class of 15 in 1908 has grown to over 300 students, with peak graduating classes of over 600 students in the late 1960s and early 1970s.

Still, the cornerstone remains, literally and figuratively, in the high school's strong community, visionary leadership, and dedicated staff. Of course the challenges are different. For this quiet, family-oriented community must thrive and co-exist within a fast-paced society and global economy.

Yet schooling, like politics, is executed locally, making the high school a broad-based preparation for citizenship: communication with and respect for others, intellectual and physical development, the building of social relationships, awareness of environmental responsibility, acquisition of craft knowledge and technical skills, exploration of artistic endeavors, promotion of healthy lifestyles and financial responsibility, and future planning. Toward these ends, Webster Groves High School remains a central agency of community development.

facing page: The Turkey Day bonfire burns to light the way to victory.

Pete Meyers' art students prepare a mural for a hallway display.

Dr. Underwood participates in the staff-student softball game.

We cherish our past. In 1866, four churches anchored public schooling in Webster Groves: the First Presbyterian Church, First Congregational Church, Emmanuel Episcopal Church, and First Baptist Church. Civic leaders convening at the Missouri Pacific Railroad Depot on Gore on August 25, 1868, made education a priority by organizing the Webster Groves School District.

Annexation of Old Orchard and Tuxedo Park (Avery) districts in 1901, the southern subdivisions in the 1930s and 1940s, and the Rock Hill District in 1948 expanded district boundaries. In 1956, the consolidation of Douglass High School in North Webster with Webster Groves High School on Selma Avenue extended the district's ethical responsibility for equal educational opportunity for all of its students. Enrollment of voluntary transfer students from St. Louis City, ensuing from a St. Louis County public schools court settlement in 1983, extended the district's horizons to include students outside the district seeking quality education.

We choose strong leaders. The district earned a reputation for superior leadership, men and women capable of articulating district goals, inspiring the school community, efficiently managing the district's resources, and earning the respect of fellow professionals. The district's superintendents became community leaders. Its high school principals, from James T. Hixson to Jon D. Clark, worked tirelessly to move the school forward while sharing decision-making with staff, students, parents, and community organizations.

We value our teachers and support staff. Aside from parents and caregivers, the district recognizes that no adults exercise more impact on the lives of students than teachers. The district's first principals were lead teachers. Many of the district's high school teachers, beginning with

The 1918 faculty pose for their yearbook picture.

Sarah J. Milligan in 1889, distinguished themselves as leaders in their fields while creating lasting traditions and extending themselves as advocates and mentors beyond the classroom.

We treasure our children. From the beginning, Webster Groves High School embraced its role as an extension of the home and the community. Mr. Hixson encouraged as many extracurricular activities as he could find faculty sponsors. Virtually every student belonged to an after-school club during the school's first four decades. Many student organizations began as Greek literary clubs patterned after college honor societies. Debating clubs, drama clubs, foreign language clubs, creative writing, yearbook, and newspaper clubs supplemented the curriculum while adding to the high school's reputation as a first-rate liberal arts institution.

Advanced Child Development students work with the future Statesmen.

While the Turkey Day football game against Kirkwood put the high school on the national map, early basketball and track teams established the high school as an athletic powerhouse, while balancing sports and academics. Basketball coach Charlie Roberts, girls' coach Dorothy Stanley, baseball coach Froebel Gaines, and football coach Ray Moss groomed Statesmen student-athletes: young men and women a "cut-above" in character, skills, and sportsmanship.

In the arts, the high school's full-scale bands, fall musicals, Little Theater plays, and second-floor art studios continue to inspire young performers and artists eighty years after Hans Lemcke brought John Philip Sousa to the high school, after Eugene Wood brought Thornton Wilder to the stage, and after the irrepressible "Miss Rep" and maestro Lemcke created musical landmarks.

The Class of 1993 cheer the start of their senior year.

The practical arts and career education also had their day. In the post–World War II era, high school principal Howard Latta predicted success not only in industrial technology and in family and consumer science courses but also in the school's highly sophisticated computer training, in its cooperative technical school program with the Special School District, and with myriad intern programs through its Community Campus Program.

Diversity makes us stronger. In the fall of 1869, Webster Groves School District established public education for African American students at the First Baptist Church and at the First Congregational Church for Caucasian students. High school "departments" followed—in 1889 at Bristol for white students and in 1925 for black students at Douglass High School in North Webster. Legal segregation continued until 1954, when the U.S. Supreme Court declared separate race-based public schools unconstitutional.

Although the academic "gap" between African American and Caucasian students might be traced in part to segregation, many Webster Groves High School graduates since the 1960s distinguished themselves scholastically and athletically, extending the legacy of Douglass High School while contributing to the success of Webster Groves High School. In addition, many voluntary desegregation transfer students in the mid-1980s arrived with an educational zeal catapulting them to high school and post-graduation success while leading to the district's awareness of St. Louis's cultural richness and diversity. Many "VTS" students figured prominently in the high school's athletic championships over the past two decades.

Community members, staff, and students prepare to canvas the neighborhoods.

We team with parents and caregivers. In a November 15, 1943, address before the high school's PTA, Willard Goslin, the district's seventh superintendent, exhorted the high school to adopt the elementary school model of parent-teacher conferences and communication.

> *We need to develop the facility and opportunities for a teacher to sit down with the parents of the children in her room and mutually become acquainted with each other, the school program, and the way in which that program is attempting to meet the needs of those children. We need an understanding and willingness to share the responsibilities of the development of the program surrounding the children of this country as we have never needed it before.*

Finally, in 1997, the high school held its first spring and fall parent-teacher conferences to supplement six-week progress reports. A high school website and e-mail access encouraged periodic two-way communication.

Volunteers get the word out on the April 2006 bond issue.

We are grateful for our community support. "This community rarely says 'no,' if it's a good cause," high school principal Jon Clark once remarked. From the passage of a $40,000 bond issue in 1905 for a new high school on Selma Avenue to a $40 million bond issue in 2006 to renovate district schools and add central air conditioning, Webster Groves School District patrons continue to recognize and support their best investment: their schools.

We care about others. The school's community service extends beyond district borders. Rarely a week or month passes without students becoming involved in outreach for the poor, hungry, or displaced. The high school's STAR service organization makes sandwiches for area food pantries. The

Statesmen volunteers travel to New Orleans to help with cleanup following Hurricane Katrina.

annual 5-K Schoemehl Run supports research for Lou Gehrig Disease. The National Honor Society continues an annual Red Cross Blood Drive. The local Special Olympics remains a school-sponsored event. Many youth groups spend spring and summer vacations building or repairing homes in depressed regions of the country. Community service or school service remains a prerequisite for many high school scholarships and awards, from the Latta Scholarship to the A+ School Program with its tutoring and mentoring component.

We work together. We are the sum of our parts. Whether through community groups or through parent, school, colleague, and student volunteers, collaboration more than competition or coexistence remains our strength as a school and as a community. Facilities and resources within and among our schools, local churches, neighboring universities, parochial schools, service institutions, fellowships, alliances, and local businesses stand readily available for the welfare of children and the benefit of citizens.

We welcome the future. As principals, staff members, teachers, and students come and go from 100 Selma Avenue, the school community thrives in the wellspring of daily lessons, in chance classmates and lifelong friends, in rounds of team sports and cocurricular activities, in the perpetual spilling in and emptying out, and in the graduation processions onto Moss Field. Left are memories, a sigh, and a smile. Here's to another 100 years!

Brad Stout and Steve Loher offer up their blood at a Red Cross blood drive.

Graduation Day for the Statesmen preschool students. Next stop: kindergarten.

Date	WG	KW	Date	WG	KW	Date	WG	KW
1907-11-28	0	5	1941-11-27	19	13	1975-11-29	15	14
1908-11-26	0	5	1942-11-26	12	12	1976-11-25	6	24
1909-11-25	W	L	1943-11-25	14	20	1977-11-24	28	7
1910-11-24	13	10	1944-11-23	0	0	1978-11-23	48	0
1911-11-23			1945-11-22	12	0	1979-11-22	28	6
1912-11-28	13	12	1946-11-28	7	6	1980-11-27	14	28
1913-11-27	5	9	1947-11-27	0	14	1981-11-26	0	7
1914-11-26			1948-11-25	7	14	1982-11-25	7	14
1915-11-25	19	6	1949-11-24	6	0	1983-11-24	12	17
1916-11-23	6	0	1950-11-23	37	0	1984-11-22	27	14
1917-11-22	76	0	1951-11-22	0	33	1985-11-29	28	11
1918-11-28			1952-11-27	0	0	1986-11-27	16	19
1919-11-21	7	0	1953-11-26	33	13	1987-11-26	0	2
1920-11-25	7	0	1954-11-25	46	7	1988-11-24		
1921-11-18	7	6	1955-11-24	7	25	1989-11-23	14	16
1922-11-23	7	6	1956-11-22	7	0	1990-11-22	9	0
1923-11-22	7	0	1957-11-28	13	27	1991-11-28	3	21
1924-11-27	**13**	**7**	1958-11-27	13	0	1992-11-26	8	6
1925-11-28	**26**	**0**	1959-11-26	13	14	1993-11-25	12	24
1926-11-27	**41**	**0**	1960-11-24	12	33	1994-11-24	13	17
1927-11-24	**6**	**0**	1961-11-23	0	7	1995-11-23	36	35
1928-11-22	6	0	1962-11-22	20	10	1996-11-28	33	12
1929-11-28	14	0	1963-11-28	0	0	1997-11-27	0	35
1930-11-27	6	8	1964-11-26	19	13	1998-11-26	14	43
1931-11-26	0	0	1965-11-25	9	0	1999-11-25	6	14
1932-11-24	0	6	1966-11-24	7	19	2000-11-23	31	9
1933-11-23	0	7	1967-11-23	12	33	2001-11-29	14	10
1934-11-22	12	6	1968-11-28	27	0	2002-11-28	14	28
1935-11-28	7	0	1969-11-27	6	0	2003-11-27	0	14
1936-11-26	14	0	1970-11-26	22	8	2004-11-25	23	24
1937-11-25	28	0	1971-11-25	23	8	2005-11-24	20	19
1938-11-24	13	6	1972-11-23	12	8	2006-11-23	28	12
1939-11-23	0	6	1973-11-22	6	7			
1940-11-28	6	12	1974-11-28	14	17			

Willard E. Goslin

Leonard A. Steger

George W. Brown

WEBSTER GROVES HIGH SCHOOL PRINCIPALS
1889-Present

1889-1905	Sarah Milligan
1905-1907	George L. Hawkins
1907-1930	James T. Hixson
1930-1931	George A. F. Hay
1931-1943	James T. Hixson
1943-1968	Howard A. Latta
1968-1969	Gerald Kusler
1969-1986	Jerry R. Knight
1986-1992	Dan Edwards
1992-1994	Yvonne Kauffman
1994-2003	Patricia Voss
2003-Present	Jon Clark

WEBSTER GROVES SCHOOL DISTRICT SUPERINTENDENTS
1889-Present

1889-1902	Sarah Milligan
1902-1914	W. D. Grove
1914-1915	H. M. Gilmore
1915-1917	William Robertson
1917-1924	Frank Hamsher
1924-1929	W. A. Gore
1929-1944	Willard E. Goslin
1944-1956	Leonard A. Steger
1956-1963	Herbert W. Schooling
1963-1981	George W. Brown
1981-1983	Jon Lokensgard
1983-1991	Max Wolfrum
1991-1992	Jerry R. Knight
1992-2001	William Gussner
2001-Present	Brent Underwood

Photo Credits

The photography for this project came from a variety of sources. Every reasonable effort to properly credit the illustrations has been made. The following organizations and individuals were of inestimable help in compiling this collection of photographs. The page numbers in which their contributions appear follow their names. When applicable, top, middle, and bottom are specified after page numbers.

Don Adams, Jr.: 95

Lee Drake: 96, 98, 101, 108

Nancy Pfitzinger: 105

Flo Ryan: 104

Urula Ruhl: 110b

St. Louis Globe-Democrat Archives of the St. Louis Mercantile Library at the University of Missouri–St. Louis: 11, 14b, 22, 44, 47, 49, 50b, 52, 60, 65b, 69

School Archives: vi, 2, 3, 4, 5, 6, 7, 8, 9, 10, 12, 13, 14t, 15, 16, 17, 18, 19t, 20, 21, 23, 24, 25t, 27, 28, 29, 30, 31, 38, 39, 41t, 42b, 45, 46, 48, 50t, 51, 53, 54, 55, 56, 58, 61, 62, 63, 64, 65t, 66, 67, 70, 71, 74, 75, 76, 77, 78, 79, 80, 81, 82, 83, 84, 85, 86, 87, 88, 89, 90, 91, 93, 94, 95, 97, 98, 99, 100, 102, 103, 108t, 109, 110, 111, 112, 113

John Shoulberg: 107

University of Missouri–St. Louis Henrietta Ambrose Collection: 34, 35, 36, 37, 40, 41b, 42t, 43

Webster Groves Historical Society: vii, 19b, 25b, 26bt, 68